WORKING WITH

ENGLISH
LANGUAGE
LEARNERS

SECOND EDITION

WORKING WITH
ENGLISH LANGUAGE LEARNERS

ANSWERS TO TEACHERS' TOP TEN QUESTIONS

SECOND EDITION

STEPHEN CARY

HEINEMANN
Portsmouth, NH

Heinemann
361 Hanover Street
Portsmouth, NH 03801–3912
www.heinemann.com

Offices and agents throughout the world

The author and publisher wish to thank those who have generously given permission to reprint borrowed material:

Cover image from *Dia's Story Cloth: The Hmong People's Journey of Freedom* by Dia Cha. Copyright © 1996. Published by Lee & Low Books. Reprinted by permission of the publisher.

Cover image from *The People Could Fly* by Leo and Diane Dillon. Copyright © 1985 by Leo and Diane Dillon. Used by permission of Alfred A. Knopf, an imprint of Random House Children's Books, a division of Random House, Inc.

Cover image from *Stone Fox* by John Reynolds Gardiner. Text copyright © 1980 by John Reynolds Gardiner. Used by permission of HarperCollins Publishers.

Bazooka Bubble Gum Packet image and Bazooka Joe comic. Reprinted by permission of The Topps Company, Inc.

Cover image from *The World Record Paper Airplane Book* by Ken Blackburn and Jeff Lammers. Copyright © 1994. Published by Workman Publishing. Reprinted by permission of the publisher.

Library of Congress Cataloging-in-Publication Data
Cary, Stephen, 1946–
    Working with English language learners : answers to teachers' top ten questions /
Stephen Cary—2nd ed.
        p. cm.
    Includes bibliographical references and index.
    Earlier ed.: Working with second language learners. 2000.
    ISBN-13: 978-0-325-00985-8 (pbk. : alk. paper)
    ISBN-10: 0-325-00985-6
    1. Language and languages—Study and teaching. 2. Second language acquistion. I. Cary, Stephen, Working with second language learners. II. Title.

P53.C286 2007
428.2'4071–dc21   2007026209

Editor: Lisa Luedeke
Production: Lynne Costa
Cover design: Jenny Jensen Greenleaf
Typesetter: Aptara, Inc.
Manufacturing: Steve Bernier

Printed in the United States of America on acid-free paper
11 10 09 08 VP   2 3 4 5

To Rich,

for thirty-five years

of friendship, music, and adventure

Contents

Acknowledgments

A big thank you . . .

To all the teachers and students who opened up their work lives, invited me in, and showed me that good coaching, like good teaching, is always a two-way street.

To the teachers who graciously provided student samples for the second edition: Teejay Bersola, Pat Dragan, Caryn Hoadley, Cheryl Namkung, and Beverly Williams.

To Lisa Luedeke, Lynne Costa, Maura Sullivan, and all the fine folks at Heinemann for their expert counsel, encouragement, and support.

To Andrea, Rebecca, Brian, Maggie, and Shep, for their patience and nuzzling while I lived in Writing & Revising Land.

A Note on the Second Edition

Since publication of the first edition in 2000, many kind readers have taken time from busy lives to email feedback on the book. Their notes of support often included a wish list for what they'd like to see in a follow-up edition. More feedback and wish list items came from my graduate students at the University of San Francisco and from teachers in my staff development workshops in the public schools. Those reader suggestions, plus the need to update terms and resources with the passage of time, drove the changes in the second edition.

The biggest change—and the one most often requested by readers—is the addition of a Discussion and Application section at the end of each chapter. Discussion questions focus on the chapter's key concepts and can be used for personal reflection or for faculty-wide dialogue. Application items ask teachers to act on the concepts, putting specific strategies and techniques to work in the classroom. Other changes and additions in the second edition include:

- updated and expanded teacher resources section
- updated and expanded reference list
- updated and expanded acronymn list
- English language learner (ELL) student samples
- teacher tools and templates
- teacher/program self-assessment charts and checklists

I'm glad to report that the heart of the book—the classroom stories and teacher coaching reflections—remains unchanged, again, per reader suggestion and consensus. And the original top ten questions are back for another run. Wherever I teach or consult, these are still the most frequently asked questions by teachers new to working with English language learners.

Thanks to everyone who offered thoughts on the first edition and shared stories of your many successes and continuing challenges in the schools.

I invite and welcome reader feedback on the second edition.

Introduction

A Near Death Experience with Staff Development

The two teachers, one a seasoned, silver-haired veteran, the other a raw, fresh-eyed beginner, cornered me at the first break in the workshop. Both were new to working with English language learners and had been "encouraged" to attend the district-wide, four-part series by the director of curriculum and instruction. The director had hyped the series as God's gift to the public schools. So the teachers came thoroughly primed to reject both presentation and presenter. And who could blame them, given the inherent teacher disrespect in mandated staff development and the extravagant claims made for the training series.

They waited until I was mid-bite into my coffee cake, then unloaded. "Look," said the vet, struggling to contain her frustration, "I've taught for more years than I want to add up, but I'm starting from scratch with second language kids. If I could only get a few basic questions answered, I'd be off and running." The newbie had more questions than his experienced colleague, but confessed he was just as borderline cranky. Give him answers to his top two or three questions and he promised to put on a happy face.

The teachers were looking at another three sessions with me on English language learner issues and declared that regardless of how nice, friendly, and "potentially competent" I might be, that was two, and probably three sessions too many—unless they could get those essential questions answered. And fast. Other teachers in the group were feeling the same, they warned. Many smelled blood. This was year one in what I hoped would be a long-term career in staff development, and so the message came through loud and clear: Answer the urgent questions immediately, or the The Guy in the Blue Blazer dies. I could kiss my budding consulting practice good-bye, and with it, any chance to help teachers help their English language learners.

After the break and my staff development epiphany, we abandoned the canned agenda and spent the rest of the morning and part of the afternoon fielding HOW DO I questions. Some questions were answered by the teachers themselves as they problem-solved in small groups. Teachers pulled from their rich backlog of experiences—in and out of the classroom—and applied what they already knew about language and content acquisition to their new population of English learners. I provided answers and food for thought here and there when needed. Along the way, we put questions on the back burner when everybody, including me, was stuck for a good, workable answer.

The workshop ended with mostly happy faces all around. I was a long way from "God's gift," joked the pair who had ambushed me earlier at the treat table, but I'd do fine, thank you. The vet, newbie, and their colleagues had gotten a good start on getting answers to the burning questions. Their experiences and problem-solving abilities had been tapped and honored. They were ready to move ahead and tackle a host of other second language acquisition theory and practice topics—topics we'd skipped earlier on the agenda. I was wearing a happy face too; maybe this whole consulting business would work out after all and I wouldn't have to get an Amway distributorship.

The Questions

A decade and a half down the line, I'm glad to report, I'm still consulting and regularly fielding teachers' questions. The ten HOW DO I questions that form the backbone of this book spring from my work with hundreds of teachers in public school districts, county offices of education, and university teacher preparation classes. The questions began as the Unmanageable Fifty, and were then boiled down to the Still Cumbersome Twenty-Five, before reaching their present incarnation as the Top Ten.

Good teaching starts with good questions. The questions here were chosen with four criteria in mind: veracity, frequency, relevancy, and difficulty. Each question on the Top Ten list is real, meaning a real teacher teaching real kids asked it. Each was asked—and asked again and again—by teachers from several grade levels who were new to working with English learners. Every question targets one of the key instructional issues teachers must address to ensure school success for their second language students. Finally, each was chosen for its level of difficulty. Questions that my attorney or the guy who tunes up my Honda can answer didn't make the list. The Top Ten:

1. How Do I assess a student's English?
2. How Do I find useful information on a student's cultural background?
3. How Do I make my spoken language more understandable?
4. How Do I get my reluctant speakers to speak English?
5. How Do I make a difficult textbook more readable?
6. How Do I help students improve their English writing?
7. How Do I teach grade-level content to English beginners?
8. How Do I help students build learning strategies?
9. How Do I support a student's first language when I don't speak the language?
10. How Do I minimize communication conflicts in a multilingual classroom?

Teacher questions often emphasize one of the four macro language skills: listening, speaking, reading, or writing. Though the book's classroom-in-action answers address particular skills, those skills are never treated in isolation. Readers, for example, will find hints on developing speaking skills in an answer dealing primarily with "writing," and hints on writing skills in another dealing primarily with "speaking." The answers' multiskill treatment reflects the reality of first and second language development. Rather than follow a neat, orderly march from listening . . . to speaking . . . to reading . . . to writing, the four skill areas interact (Freeman and Freeman 1998) and are part of a common "linguistic data pool" (Harste, Woodward, and Burke 1984). Language acquisition is more a matter of get-this-*with*-that, than get-this-*then*-that; it comes in wholes, not pieces. Similarly, teacher questions sometimes separate language and content and appear to imply that language learning must precede academic learning. Like the four macro language skills, language and content are interdependent and mutually enhancing. Students can and do learn language through content and content through language (Krashen 2003; Díaz-Rico and Weed 2006). Each classroom story in the book illustrates this critical language-content link.

Who You Are

You're a K–12 preservice-teacher, teacher, or resource teacher who's new to working with English language learners. You want fast, practical, real-world answers to help kids learn language and content. You're a self-starter who can take the instructional ball and run with it when given a minimum of good direction. Or you're an administrator or school board member wanting a quick overview of key English language learner issues your hardworking and badly underpaid teachers are wrestling with daily. Or you're my mom, who buys anything I write.

Who the Students Are

The book focuses on the five million plus English language learners now in American schools. ELL numbers continue to expand at a dizzying rate. Since the first edition of this book in 2000, K–12 schools have enrolled an additional 430,000 nonnative English speakers. From 1993 to 2004, English language learner enrollment increased by a little over 65 percent. Schools in fourteen states, including Oregon, Colorado, Nebraska, Indiana, Arkansas, Alabama, and North Carolina, each experienced growth greater than 200 percent. By comparison, in the same period, the enrollment of native English speakers grew by only a little over 5 percent (U.S. Department of Education 2005).

Nationwide, one in every ten students is an English language learner. In California, it's one in four (California Department of Education 2006). These students enter U.S. schools with a treasure trove of first languages: 384 at last count. Here's the top ten ranking by number of speakers:

1. Spanish
2. Vietnamese
3. Hmong
4. Cantonese
5. Korean
6. Haitian Creole
7. Arabic
8. Russian
9. Tagalog
10. Navajo

Though nearly 80 percent of the students speak Spanish as a first language, other heritage languages include everything from Arapaho, Farsi, Ibo, and Mien to Punjabi, Samoan, Thai, Uzbek, and Zapoteco. Our English language learners may be newly arrived immigrants from any of a hundred different countries, or U.S.-born children from homes where a language other than English is usually spoken. The students may be square one beginners in English or have good English oral skills and a moderate amount of English literacy. Some enter the system with strong academic skills; others enter with weaker skills because of minimal schooling in the home country.

Regardless of their differences, all second language students have two critical needs: language and access. They need to become fluent, communicatively competent speakers and proficient readers and writers of English. And they need access to the core curriculum to gain content knowledge, critical thinking skills, and learning-for-life strategies. The two needs are inextricably linked: More second language makes for more access, and more access makes for more second language. Neither is a luxury, take-it-or-leave-it item. Students' success in school and their later success in the marketplace require top-notch English and top-notch academic skills. Get those skills and do well; miss them and lots of luck.

Though the book targets K–12 English language learners, nearly all activities, strategies, and techniques advocated here are appropriate for native English speakers as well. Extracting information from the visuals in a textbook chapter before hitting the print, using artifacts to make a unit on the Civil War more lively and understandable, or showing a DVD as a "scene setter" for a trade book read-aloud, are effective instructional practices that make more learning for *all* kids—not just English language learners.

A Note on Terms

Many of the labels historically given to children who enter school with few or no English skills carry a decidedly negative connotation. The *limited* in LES/NES (Limited/Non-English Speaking) or LEP/NEP (Limited/Non-English Proficient) emphasizes what students are missing rather than what they have: primary language and developing second language skills. Choosing a more positive and serviceable term is no easy matter. Some terms are positive but awkward like LCD (Linguistically and Culturally Diverse) or SAE (Student Acquiring English). Other terms are positive but potentially fuzzy. For example, both ELL (English Language Learner) and ELD (English Language Development) could apply to all students in the American school system, since all are involved in perfecting English language skills. And ELD, like ESL (English as a Second Language), often refers to a particular type of instruction, not just a particular type of student.

Even the term I've favored for many years, SLL (Second Language Learner), has problems. After all, communicative-based second language teachers help students *acquire* rather than learn language. And some of our "second" language learners are actually learning English as a third or fourth language. Unfortunately, any term we might choose will be less than perfect.

Over the past several years, ELL has gradually supplanted other labels and is now the dominant term in local, state, and federal documents, educational literature, and teacher lounges around the country. The book's title change, from the first edition's *Working with Second Language Learners* to the present *Working with English Language Learners*, reflects the preeminent position of the ELL term. Though I emphasize the term in the new edition, you'll still find me occasionally using SLL, my old favorite. The terms are synonymous and interchangeable throughout the book.

What the Book Gives You

If you're hoping for definitive answers to all your questions about English language learner instruction, take a deep breath. The book provides fundamental information and a number of vital tricks of the ELL trade that you can immediately apply in the classroom—as in tomorrow—but it does not work miracles, or even try to. Each chapter deals with a single HOW DO I question and includes five parts: the question, a reader's guide, a classroom story, my coaching reflections, and a closing discussion and application section. The questions are short, pointed, and written in plain, jargon-free English. Their no-nonsense tone reflects the real tone of the questions when asked in workshops and teacher coaching sessions. The reader's guide pinpoints the story's central issue and summarizes the key ideas threading through the story that help the reader answer the HOW DO I question. The guide also provides an overview of the story, including academic content, grade, teacher experience, type of school, and student languages.

The stories carry the reader into the classroom to watch and listen to how other teachers have answered the same questions. All the stories are real, collected along the public school consulting trail over the past fifteen years. All are composites to some degree, however, combining elements from more than one classroom in order to spotlight a larger number of strategies and techniques. I also add several dramatic, but transparent, embellishments here and there for narrative punch. Finally, consistent with the confidential nature of the coaching process, all student, teacher, and school names are inventions.

The classroom stories reflect effective, research-informed practices. They offer good answers to the HOW DO I questions but not complete answers, and certainly not the only answers. You'll need more information, more think-time, and more try-it-out teaching time for fuller answers, answers that are tailor-made to your instructional style and students. Moreover, answers to how-do-I-teach questions naturally change in relation to new research findings and practitioner reports. Check back with me in a few years and I may offer somewhat different classroom stories and therefore somewhat different answers to the same questions.

The story answers simply provide a reasonable—and reasoned—starting point. The classroom stories invite readers to construct meaning on their own, to make the conceptual, grade-level, or subject matter leaps needed to connect the story to themselves and their own classroom of kids. Though the stories are grade specific, the issues, strategies, and techniques within the stories often aren't. A kindergarten teacher, for example, may find a number of useful hints in a story pegged for middle school youngsters. In like manner, the middle school teacher may be surprised—but delighted—to find applicable strategies in a primary grade story. Readers comfortable getting answers by a show-me-in-the-flesh modeling process will call the story section home.

The reflections that follow each classroom story pinpoint best practices, lay out the rationale for why teacher and students did what they did, and offer spin-off strategies and techniques. They offer a personal, teacher coach view, but like the stories, are research-informed. Each is underpinned by a theoretical framework with principles pulled from a variety of sources, including communicative language teaching, constructivism, bilingual/biliteracy education, progressive literacy, critical pedagogy, process writing, collaborative learning, brain-based teaching, SDAIE (Specially Designed Academic Instruction in English), and CALLA (Cognitive Academic Language Learning Approach).

The reflections sections are more directive. I preach a bit, but I do it on the smallest soapbox I can find. Readers who live for extended education courses over summer vacation and are comfortable getting answers by a "telling" process will spend more time here. Most readers, however, will find that the combination of story and coaching reflections makes for more powerful learning.

Finally, each chapter ends with a Discussion and Application section. The discussion questions target vital English language learner issues and are designed to spark personal reflection and lively, problem-solving dialogue among colleagues. Each application item invites teachers to pull an important activity, strategy, or technique from the chapter story and try it out in the real world of the classroom.

Getting the Most out of the Book

Each chapter is built to stand alone. Zero in on questions you really want answers to and fly past those you've already got answers to. This read it or skip it approach means you can get what you need from the book quickly. And without guilt; good readers skip like crazy, so skip away.

Many readers may find they get a lot more from the book when it's read with a colleague or as a text selection for faculty-wide study sessions. Buddy or group reading and discussion—using the end-of-chapter questions as a guide—provide alternative perspectives and let you think out loud, clarify concepts, pose additional questions, and trade solutions to common instructional problems.

Beyond the Book

Finding information you need and finding it fast is no easy matter given the size and complexity of the literature on second language acquisition theory, practice, and materials. The References and Resources sections at the end of the book will help make the info hunt a lot easier. Each book, article, and website can help you answer additional questions about English language learner issues. Thankfully, none requires major search and scrounge time to locate; you can find any listed resource with a quick phone call or an even quicker mouse click.

Let's start. Strap a couple big suction cups on your feet and join me in the classrooms for some fly-on-the-wall watching and listening. Enjoy.

1

How do I assess a student's English?

READER'S GUIDE
English Language Learner Issue: Language assessment

Key Ideas
- Rely on authentic, performance-based assessment
- Develop multiple-source, "big package" assessment
- View assessment as an ongoing process
- Understand the terrors and limitations of formal language testing
- Use observation, chats, and anecdotal notes

Content:	Engineering/bookcase project
Grade:	3
Teacher Experience:	6 years
ELL Language(s):	Spanish
School:	K–5, suburban

The Classroom Story

Break-in Time

Day four and still no English from Amalia. That's not quite accurate, thought Lisa, as she watched her new third grader scoot a chair into a collaborative work circle. Amalia had spoken some English here and there, she recalled, thinking back over the little girl's first few days in class, but nothing substantial, mostly automatic courtesy phrases and a few short responses to questions about favorite activities away from school.

Amalia was really not talking, not conversing in English—with the teacher or with any of the kids. Her lack of English conversation couldn't be due to shyness, Lisa decided. She chatted readily in Spanish with two bilingual classmates. Maybe the English simply wasn't there. But this didn't square with information found in the cum folder. Amalia had been in the U.S. nearly ten months, with six months of schooling in El Paso and two in San Diego before enrolling at Ellington. She had to have more English than this, the teacher believed. But how much more?

Formal language testing would help answer the question. Like each new English language learner to the district, Amalia would be given the LAS (Language Assessment Scales), a normed and state-approved oral and written proficiency test in English. But it would be another two weeks, per Lisa's request, before Amalia took the LAS, and a week beyond that before the teacher received the test results.

Lisa made sure each new ELL student coming into class was given at least two weeks of "break-in" time before being tested. Other English language learners at Ellington were tested within two days of enrollment. Lisa's strong opposition to the principal's unwritten "instant testing policy" had made her somewhat less than popular in district administrative circles. The principal had always granted the postponement requests, but done so reluctantly, each time decrying what he believed to be a serious loss of critical, baseline test data. Lisa was convinced the man would test students on the bus as they rode to school their first day, if he could only work out the logistics. With formal testing on the back burner, Lisa was on her own in answering the critical "how much English?" question.

Amalia settled into the work circle and sat beside a bilingual classmate. The two girls conversed in Spanish for a few seconds and then gathered tape, scissors, rulers, and sheets of thin cardboard for their group from a central supply table. Amalia's spoken English remained a mystery, but not her comprehension of oral English. The girl had few problems understanding basic class activity directions. And she had grasped many of the questions kids asked about her life in Mexico during the first day "getting to know you" chat. Only a few questions needed to be repeated or reformulated with simpler constructions and terms. Amalia answered the questions in Spanish that day and bridged to the teacher and other students through a bilingual classmate.

OK, Lisa noted, so her understanding of conversational English is so-so, maybe a two on a five-point scale, where one equals beginning-level comprehension and five equals advanced. Given that level of oral comprehension and the time and schooling here, Lisa guessed that Amalia spoke more English, though, again, she wasn't sure how much more. Additional kid-watching and a little more note-taking might help fill in the information holes.

Four-Box Assessment

Lisa favored a minimalist approach to note-taking. Her rule of thumb was simple: Document only the bare essentials, in this case, what Amalia could *do* with English. She made notes and recorded samples of language on a single sheet of paper divided into four boxes, each box labeled with one of the broad language skill areas: listening, speaking, reading, and writing. A scale line ran across the top of each box where she circled a number between one and five to quantify her estimate of Amalia's language comprehension and production.

Amalia was working with five other students on a building project, exploring the load-carrying capacity of cardboard columns of different lengths, thicknesses, and shapes. The project was sparked by the classroom need for additional book storage and one student's simple "I wonder . . ." question: "I wonder if we could make our own bookcases?" Lisa checked in to see if Amalia's group needed an "engineering consultation." Nope. No problems. She joined the kids on the floor to learn if the budding engineers were on target as much as they thought they were. The kids were posing questions, hypothesizing, testing their column constructions, calculating dimensions and load totals, and recording results. Looked like the modeling she did in the morning paid off; the group was on task and moving along nicely. How about Amalia, though? Still quiet. Nothing on the English talk front. I'd hang back too, thought Lisa, without much second language to work with.

One boy taped up a twenty-centimeter-long column and readied it for a load test. The group's squared column had collapsed at five wooden blocks. The group hypothesized that the rounded column would structurally fail at four. Students took turns gingerly stacking blocks on top of the column. Three blocks. Four. Five blocks and holding. "Six!" Amalia suddenly yelled out. "We can put in six!" Amalia jumped to her feet, her long black hair flying in all directions. She grabbed a block and waved it in the air. "Let's do . . . more, put in six blocks! Come on, this now! This thing is . . . hold six and I know and we put seven . . . and . . . maybe and this thing is shape good of the . . . and . . . round, the round is good and not the kinds . . . with square up this sides. Who is thinking put six? I know the round hold six! OK?" The group gave Amalia the go-ahead for another block. "Look!" Amalia added the sixth block and the column held. "Let's put . . . do seven!"

As the language exploded out of Amalia, Lisa's eyebrows lifted and she smiled. Bingo. So Amalia talked. And talked up a storm! Granted, she was making lots of errors with pronunciation, syntax, and prepositions. She was often struggling to find the right words, but she was communicating, getting her basic points across. In the speaking section of the four-box assessment sheet, Lisa recorded a couple of Amalia's comments and circled a three on the five-point scale. Before the bookcase activity, she would have given her a two. But what about English literacy?

Amalia jotted down the latest column measurements and load test data. Without help from her groupmates, she fit all the information into the right spots on the teacher-provided data sheet. Good, thought Lisa. She's reading the headings, and reading them correctly. The teacher consulted with the other engineering teams working around the room, then checked back with Amalia's group. Students were discussing their load test experiments and giving data to the group writer, who recorded information for the final design report. Amalia shared, but her points lacked the length and descriptive depth of points made by native English speakers. The group's design report would include a summary and analysis of results and a detailed diagram of the group's proposed construction. Lisa would review the design, make suggestions if needed, and then give the group the green light to build its bookcase.

Lisa asked Amalia to read some of what she had written in her experiment log. Her writing was full of nonstandard spellings and convoluted syntax—"colap bloc fas don in 3 and drop; drop esquar fas by long 10 centi. aguin don in 4 test"—but she was able to report the basics of what had transpired in the group's several load test experiments. Again, as with oral English, she got her points across, but this time not as clearly. At the teacher's request, Amalia also read data summaries from two students now busy preparing for the next load test. The girl understood most of what she read, but read haltingly, stumbling on more words than when reading her own log. All the data summaries were short. How was Amalia doing with longer stretches of reading and writing? Unfortunately, there was nothing much to go on at this point: Amalia had not produced anything longer than the summaries. Given her difficulty with the summaries, however, Lisa felt that longer pieces of English reading and writing might be tough to impossible for Amalia—at least for awhile. Lisa gave Amalia a two out of five for English literacy and circled the corresponding number on the reading and writing box scales.

The engineering groups disbanded after a large group sharing of results, and Amalia and the other students moved into fifteen minutes of independent journal writing. Amalia's journal quickly filled with line after line of Spanish. Lisa stopped and knelt at Amalia's table and told the girl what a great writer she was in Spanish. "I can read a little Spanish, but I wish I could understand this more!" Lisa confessed. Amalia talked to the teacher about "crazy" Aunt Nica, whose silly antics now stood immortalized on the journal page. One of Amalia's bilingual table buddies translated the Aunt Nica tale for the teacher. Lisa laughed and told Amalia that Aunt Nica "sounds a lot like my sister!"

Making Sense of the Boxes

Later, as the kids headed off to lunch, Lisa reviewed her notes and summed up what she had learned about Amalia's second language proficiency. Listening? A two on the five-point, zilch-to-advanced scale, with comprehension better on the family questions than the design activity questions. Speaking? A three, though that could be a notch high, Lisa reflected; Amalia struggled for words a lot and teacher and groupmates occasionally struggled to understand her points about the bookcase construction experiments. Reading and writing? A two, though she would like some additional data to feel secure with the two.

Lisa considered the mile markers along the developmental language highway—beginning, early intermediate, intermediate, early advanced, advanced, and native-level fluency—and pegged Amalia at early intermediate. At least, that was the determination right now. She reminded herself that today's answers to the "how much English?" question could change as she observed Amalia in other activities requiring different kinds and amounts of conversational and academic English.

Lisa sat at her desk and hurriedly unpacked a tuna sandwich and a bag of chips. She had twenty minutes to eat and use the restroom, ten if she returned a call from one of the students' parents. She thought about Amalia and all the work that lay ahead—for student and teacher alike. Moving Amalia down the road to better oral and literacy skills would require loads of activities like the bookcase/math/science project—high-interest activities across the curriculum where Amalia would want to use, and hence improve, her English. Good activities took time to plan, something Lisa never had enough of during the regular school week.

As students rolled back in from lunch, she opened her desk calendar to the coming weekend and slowly scratched through "Napa Wine Tour." Below the scratched-out words, Lisa wrote "PLANNING" and underlined it twice.

Saturday would look a little different now. She and husband, Marv, would pop open a bottle of cheap Chablis and maybe play some Ping-Pong in the garage. But Napa could wait; Amalia and the other kids couldn't.

⟿⟾

Reflections

The Instant Testing Welcome

Not all issues warrant a fight with the Administrative Powers That Be. Going to the mat for an after-school archery program or a new staff room copier may not be worth it. Fighting tooth and nail for good assessment, however, always is. Lisa's small but courageous act of rebellion in refusing to have Amalia immediately tested was smart on two counts. First, it ensured more humane testing. Imagine yourself—as an adult—entering a new country and a new school. Maybe you're spending a summer abroad and have enrolled in a university course for foreign teachers to learn Spanish or Arabic or Mandarin.

On your first day, a strange woman enters the classroom, pulls you out, and walks you down the hall and into a small room. You sit at a table and begin a long battery of tests in a language you don't know. The woman is smiling. Her voice is soft and her manner gentle. She assures you several times that you're doing terrific on the tests, but you know you're getting most everything wrong—the listening part, the speaking part, and the reading and writing parts. You're bombing the works. You freeze. You *know* you know a little something of the language, but you can't even get that out. Despite the tester's congenial demeanor, you feel apprehensive and uncomfortable, and a bit ashamed. You think you should know more, do better. Maybe you're a little stupid with language. Or maybe just a little stupid, period. Now imagine all that at eight or nine years old. Lisa believed instant testing wasn't the warmest welcome Ellington School could give Amalia, or any child for that matter.

Second, Lisa's opposition to instant formal testing was smart because it ultimately produced more accurate test results. Two weeks down the line, when Amalia took the LAS, she was a lot more comfortable with school. She had made friends and felt safer. She had met and visited with the testing person a few days before the test. Moreover, Amalia had learned from the teacher and her classmates what the LAS was all about—finding out where kids are with their second language—and more importantly, what the test wasn't about—grades and intelligence. Amalia relaxed on the test and hence was able to do her best.

But formal testing instruments are a lot like police dogs: They sniff out what they're built to sniff out. Dogs on a narcotics squad will pass up burgers, steaks, chops, and cats to find cocaine. In like manner, formal tests will often pass up considerable amounts of language in order to target the specific, say a particular noun. A student shown a picture of a submarine and asked to name it, for example, might respond with, "a long boat with the rockets and for dive in water and is use on war and get secrets." That's a great answer, but would be counted wrong on a formal test's vocabulary section; the only correct response is "submarine." The child's strong concept of submarine and the language used to convey that concept goes unrecorded, uncounted, and unappreciated.

In another section of most formal language proficiency tests, a student listens to a story and is then asked to retell it in his or her own words. The story retelling attempts to spark more holistic, open-ended language, and hence avoid the problems of discrete point, one-right-answer items. Unfortunately, few kids are excited by the formal test stories, which are notoriously bland and drop out of left field into their laps. Students are unlikely to want to actively listen to and retell unengaging stories, especially to someone obviously testing their retelling and who they suspect has heard the story a hundred times before. There is no motivation, no real communication need for the student to "go deep" into what may well be a rich—or at least richer—stockpile of second language. The language a student uses for retelling, therefore, may be less than what the student really has available.

Real Life for Real Language

Despite the shortcomings, formal tests can provide valuable data for teachers about a student's second language skills. For example, the LAS may have pinpointed Amalia's difficulties in distinguishing specific English phonemes or problems with comparative adjectives—language "cracks" that need filling for better communication. And good formal tests like the LAS, IPT (IDEA Proficiency Test), or CELDT (California English Language Development Test) make an admirable attempt through picture description and stories to determine students' ability with oral discourse—stretches of spoken language longer than a sentence.

But Lisa understood the limitations of formal tests. She knew that authentic language assessment required something few tests ever elicit from kids—lots of authentic language. Looking at how Amalia processed and used language in real-life settings where she had a genuine need to communicate, as in the bookcase-building activity, gave Lisa what she was after—a better sense of what Amalia could and could not do with English. For example, Lisa knew Amalia could do a short oral report on upcoming earthquake experiments, something she never would have asked the girl to do before the bookcase engineering observation. A written report on earthquakes still wasn't in the cards, but little by little.

Lisa had the art of kid-watching and kid-talking down flat. She was able to keep the class running smoothly, play the engineering consultant role, listen and creatively respond to group questions, and at the same time attend to and make notes regarding Amalia's language strengths and weaknesses. Throughout her interaction with Amalia, Lisa kept the focus squarely on bookcase design. The teacher was after naturally produced language and got it for three reasons. One, something about the design activity clicked with Amalia. She found it meaningful and enticing enough to make her want to use her second language. Two, Amalia's few days of settling-in time had allowed her to gain the confidence and comfort level she needed to risk speaking a language she was far from proficient in. And three, the teacher chose to talk with Amalia rather than test her. Real talking makes for real talk; testing makes for test talk. And talk is to test talk like a home-cooked meal is to a frozen dinner. A Swanson® pot pie is still food—but just barely.

Big Package Assessment

Authentic assessment is a process, not a one-shot event; it requires multiple measures of student performance over time (O'Malley and Pierce 1996). That's why Lisa planned on ongoing observations, chats, and note-taking with Amalia throughout the rest of the school year. She knew the answer to the "how much English?" question would likely change by late afternoon and for sure by next week. Kids, after all, don't stand still with a second language. She also knew she only had part of the answer to the "how much English RIGHT NOW?" question, though admittedly a significant and helpful part. A student's quantity and quality of second language can vary with the activity, setting, number of participants, participant relationships, academic demands, and language response time provided (Ellis 1986; Foster and Skehan 1996). In a different activity that same day, Lisa may have found that Amalia had even more English, for example, comprehension of a number of idioms picked up from favorite TV shows.

Good assessment is a package deal. And the bigger the package, the better the assessment. In the months following her initial appraisal, Lisa hooked ongoing observations and chats with Amalia to periodic reviews of the girl's portfolio and project work—all part of language-in-use, performance-based assessment. Additional data were gleaned from more formal language testing and her cum folder. Visits with parents and siblings shed light on Amalia's language development in Spanish and English away from school. This mix of assessment sources helped Lisa develop an accurate and evolving picture of what Amalia could do with her second language. That knowledge, in turn, was used to set high but realistic learning goals with the girl. Finally, the "how much English?" answers from big package assessment told Lisa to what degree activities had to be modified to make them "language doable" and, hence, educationally profitable for Amalia.

Postscript

In one of our early coaching sessions, Lisa and I sat in the Ellington staff lounge, drinking coffee, and played the "Fast Forward" game. Fifteen years down the line we saw Amalia working as an architect or perhaps as an engineer for NASA. Lisa would still be championing authentic assessment and ruffling the occasional administrative feather. And both of us saw the principal, clear as day, living in a retirement community in central Florida, instant-testing each new resident on the intricacies of the Medicare system.

Discussion and Application

Discussion

1. Reflect on your school's formal language-testing environment for English learners. How emotionally comfortable are students with the testing? Consider enrollment-to-test timeline, venue, testing personnel, test content and procedures, and what information (if any) students are given about the test before being tested. Mark an X where the school falls on the continuum in Figure 1–1.

If you've pegged your school anywhere between hostile and neutral, what elements could you modify—without invalidating the test or losing your job!—to lower student anxiety and improve overall comfort level?

2. How useful are your formal language test results? To what degree do they help you pinpoint language strengths and weaknesses, modify

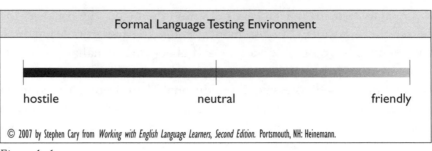

Figure 1–1.

curriculum and instruction, and make your program more effective for English language learners? Stated more irreverently: Does formal language proficiency testing benefit students or simply help your school label kids and comply with state and federal mandates?

3. Think about the strategies Lisa used with Amalia to informally answer the "how much English?" question. What strategies are you currently using for authentic, language-in-action assessment? What else do you need to do—observations, note-taking, portfolio and project review, parent interviews, student self-assessments—to put the "big" in big package assessment? Is there an additional strategy or two you'd recommend to Lisa to make her second language assessment even more broad-based and effective?

Application

1. If you're unfamiliar with your school's formal language proficiency instrument—get familiar! Ask one of the Powers That Be at the district office to walk you through the test. Find out what the test measures and, just as important, what it doesn't.

How much of the test uses a discrete point or sentential-based approach, measuring language in small, decontextualized pieces? Examples might include having students distinguish between the phonemes /v/ and /b/, identifying the correct placement of adjectives, or choosing between present and past progressive tenses in a series of unconnected sentences.

How much of the test uses a more holistic, discourse-based approach, measuring language in larger, contextualized units with more clues and cues in place? Examples might include having students respond orally to

questions posed in different social situations, filling in the correct pronouns and verbs in a cloze-type (deleted word) newspaper story, or writing
a coherent paragraph based on a topic of personal interest.

2. Choose one of your second language learners for a four-box assessment
(Figure 1–2), perhaps someone you suspect has more English than formal

Student's Name: Angel
Grade: 3rd
Primary Language: Spanish

Date:
Lesson:
Grouping:

ELL Language Assessment

Listening
Level: (Beginning) 1 – 2 –③– 4 – 5 (Advanced)
Teacher (T) poses the question –
"Look at your paper, and see if you
can find 'Jupiter.'"
Angel (A): Number 4
T: What else are we missing?
A: Neptune! Neptune!

T: What are you supposed to do?
A: Color | M (another student):
T: Color what? | What color is Neptune?
A: The planets. | A: Neptune? Azul.

Speaking
Level: (Beginning) 1 – 2 –③– 4 – 5 (Advanced)
ST (student teacher) asks, "What's
this?" (pointing at his (Angel's)
drawing of the solar system.
A: It's the milky way.
ST: Milky way?
A: Yes. Right here.
J (Another student): No, it's the asteroid
belt.
A: The what?
J: The asteroid belt
A: Oh yeah. the aster...
(While getting ready to go outside...)
A: I don't got a jacket.

Reading
Level: (Beginning) 1 – 2 –③– 4 – 5 (Advanced)
Reads his journal entry dated
October 14, 2005. (Phonetic
spelling)... had difficulty
"reading" his own writing...
"en ori talyu dad my llav
quifest." Rereads this three
times, and shakes his head
and says, "I don't know this."
Reads a teacher's response to
his journal. Angel does a
great job reading his teacher's

Writing
Level: (Beginning) 1 –②– 3 – 4 – 5 (Advanced)
See journal entry...
"Ticher yuo laik to hi
ey tiche yicas I want
to bi I ticher went
ay crou napa I want to
vi ey ticher oey
polismean."
(phonetic spelling.)

Notes: writing fluently.

Figure 1–2. Four-box assessment. Grade 3 ELL, early intermediate/intermediate, The Language Academy of Sacramento (LAS), Sacramento, California. LAS is a two-way Spanish immersion charter school. Teacher: Teejay Bersola.

test results indicate. Often, the quiet, fade-into-the-background kids are the best candidates. Assess the student over a span of two or three days. Remember Lisa's minimalist approach: record small samples of second language, not tons of it. Keep the focus on language-in-use rather than language-in-testing, on what the student is doing (or wants to do) with English in a variety of authentic, communicative settings.

Analyze the data for language needs, then adjust some aspect of curriculum and instruction to meet one or more of those needs. What additional information would you like regarding the quantity and quality of this student's second language? How will you get it?

3. Assessment in L1 (primary language) is essential for establishing language dominance and sorting out possible learning disabilities from perfectly routine second language deficits (Artiles and Ortiz 2002). Find out if your English language learners have been assessed in their primary language and ask for the results. Were multiple assessment sources used or only a formal, standardized instrument? If L1 assessment is absent or inadequate, formally advocate for its inclusion or improvement. Letter to the principal or school board, anyone?

2

How do I find useful information on a student's cultural background?

READER'S GUIDE
English Language Learner Issue: Cultural learning/application

Key Ideas
- Use multiple sources
- Learn a student's "outside" story
- Identify potential cultural conflict points
- Know basic first and second language differences and similarities
- Avoid common cultural learning pitfalls

Content:	Family history stories
Grade:	5
Teacher Experience:	2 years
ELL Language(s):	Hmong, Spanish
School:	K–8, rural

The Classroom Story

Mystery Boy

Lenny Rossovich was almost out of the classroom when the phone rang with a message from the school secretary. He was getting a new student tomorrow. The boy's name was Ka or Kas, and he spoke "some" English. And he was Asian. The secretary apologized, but that was it—all the info the office had right now on the new fifth grader. Stay tuned.

Knowing the boy was Asian, Lenny thought on the drive home, was about as helpful as knowing somebody's footwork was dancing. What sort of dancing were we talking? Tap? Ballet? Swing? Hip-Hop? Salsa? Asia made up nearly a third of the world's land area. The new student might be from any number of countries within that enormous expanse—China, Vietnam, Laos, Cambodia, Malaysia, maybe Indonesia. And within those large political divisions, the boy might be from any one of several dozen ethnic groups. *Asian* was a convenient, one-size-fits-all label, but a starting point only.

In the morning, Ka Xiong arrived at Fitzgerald School with his mom and two older aunts. The women spoke little English and could provide Lenny with few details beyond the boy's name and age and something about schooling and family in Fresno. Based on the name, physical traits, and the colorfully embroidered clothing worn by the women, Lenny guessed Ka was Southeast Asian. Kids introduced themselves and welcomed Ka to the classroom. Some asked the new boy questions. Ka told everyone he was from Laos and that he was Hmong, which Lenny wrote as *Mung* on the board. He had gone to school for about a year and a half in Fresno and liked pizza and basketball. As the questions continued, Ka's answers grew shorter and less audible. The boy was clearly uncomfortable and Lenny quickly ended the group questioning. At this point, Lenny knew more about Ka than the day before, but not by much. He wanted a lot more information on the small, dark-haired boy who wouldn't look him in the eye and remained silent through most of the afternoon. "Mung" had thrown both kids and teacher for a loop. Who on earth were the "Mung"?

After school, Lenny sat at his desk staring at a pile of student journals and free-associated. Mung . . . Mung bean. Nope. Mung . . . ming. Ming Dynasty. Nope—wrong country. Ming . . . Ming the Merciless from Flash Gordon. Wrong planet! He was going no place fast. Lenny checked Ka's enrollment form in the office. Information on the form was sketchy and had been dictated by Ka's mom to one of the school secretaries. The *Asian* box was checked under Student's Ethnicity. Lenny sighed. OK, this we know. Country of Birth: Laos. This we know, too. In the Home Language Survey section, each question had the same response: "Mong." Lenny shook his head. Mung or Mong?

In the school library, Lenny found a reference book on Southeast Asians, looked up Laos, and soon discovered that *Mung* was actually *Hmong*. *Hmong* referred to both a people and their language. Originally from Southwestern China, the Hmong settled in the mountainous country of northern Laos, Vietnam, and Thailand in the early 1800s. At the end of the Vietnam War, thousands fled the killing fields of Laos and waited years in crowded Thai refugee camps before receiving permission to enter the U.S. Lenny quickly skimmed through several more pages and closed the book. Lots of interesting history there, but he needed more than history. He logged on to one of the library's Internet computers and rocketed off to cyberspace. A quick Googling of "Hmong" produced over two million hits. A Web page called "The Hmong Tragedy" that discussed the Hmong and the CIA caught Lenny's eye. What was that all about? He bookmarked it for a later click. What he needed now was information to help him work more effectively with Ka and Ka's family—as in tomorrow. The CIA cloak-and-dagger story would have to wait.

Lenny wanted the basics on Hmong beliefs and customs. Where were the potential conflict points between Hmong and American mainstream culture? What specific aspects of an American fifth-grade class might Ka and his family find puzzling or troublesome? And he particularly wanted to know how the Hmong language compared to English. What English sounds or structures would Ka find unusually difficult? What elements did the two languages have in common that would make English acquisition a little easier?

Lenny narrowed the search, adding "teaching" to "Hmong," and cut the hits to a little under 350,000. Including "English" as a third keyword dropped the total to about 250,000—still enough information for two lifetimes. He scrolled quickly through several pages of results but couldn't find the practical, teacher-oriented help he was after. In frustration, he back-buttoned to page 1, determined to give the first few results a more thorough check, and suddenly, bingo, the mother lode: The Hmong Homepage (http://www.hmongnet.org/), a vast storehouse of net-based resources on Hmong culture, language, history, and current resettlement issues, created by two graduate students at the University of Minnesota with contributions from a number of Hmong students and K–12 ESL teachers. From The Hmong Homepage, Lenny followed links to the Southeast Asia Resource Action Center, the Hmong Times Newspaper, the Talking Hmong/English Dictionary, and finally landed on a page called Educational Resources and Lesson Plans from the Hmong Cultural Center in Saint Paul.

He spent more than two hours online, locating promising sites, and skimming documents. At home, Lenny went back on the Web for a few Hmong language lessons, complete with audio samples. Even though Hmong and English shared the same basic subject-verb-object syntax, the differences were striking. Most Hmong words were only one syllable long, and each syllable required a single tone—and only that tone out of a possible eight—to give it meaning. Change the tone of the syllable and you changed the word. Other tricky elements: Hmong lacked inflected forms, and instead used word order and word combinations to indicate number, tense, gender, and possession. The language also used a host of noun classifiers that were nonexistent in English to denote class membership. And it loved serial verbs, which in English might look like: I went walked bought milk. Traveling from English to Hmong would be tough; traveling from Hmong to English would be just as tough, and for Ka, tougher since he would also be dealing with considerable cultural conflict, according to the Web sources.

Peer Buddies

Three weeks later, Ka sat beside Emilio, Room Seventeen's peer buddy extraordinaire. Emilio was the best of the best when it came to working collaboratively with his classmates, especially with those classmates other kids found particularly difficult. And he was Lenny's number one choice for easing new students into the classroom, answering their questions and helping them learn the rules and regs and daily routine. Lenny marveled at the way Emilio was able to "read" people and fashion a response with just the right words and tone to advance a conversation or strengthen a fragile ego. Emilio might be a major washout in math this year, thought Lenny, but his social-emotional IQ was off the chart. The boy's patience and persistence in getting through to people made him particularly effective with English language learners, and Lenny had hooked him with Ka almost immediately.

Lenny watched while Emilio explained something related to the family history storyboards kids were working on. A pure verbal explanation in English wasn't working. Ka looked a little lost, just as he looked that first day when kids and teacher asked him questions about Laos. Emilio pointed to the first and last panels on his own storyboard and verbally labeled the panels "beginning" and "ending." Not sure if Ka fully understood, Emilio added, "Here's where my story is going to start and here's where my story is going to end—it stops here." Ka nodded his head and thanked his peer buddy. He either understood—or he was just being polite to Emilio. Lenny wasn't sure. In fact, there was still a lot about Ka and the Hmong Lenny wasn't sure about. There was a lot to learn. But he was learning and so was the class, which was about half Latino kids of

Mexican and El Salvadoran heritage and half African American and white. The Web sources helped. So did books provided by the children's librarian at the public library. Several of the books on Laos and the Hmong became popular items at free reading time, and kids sometimes found a picture or fact in the books that sparked a question and a conversation with Ka.

Story Connections

A class favorite and the book that produced the most questions was *Dia's Story Cloth: The Hmong People's Journey to Freedom*, by Dia Cha (1996). Storycloths, called *pa'ndau* or *flower cloth* in Hmong, were first developed in the Thai refugee camps and combine two strong Hmong traditions, oral storytelling and fine needlework. The craft has continued in the Hmong community in the U.S., and the cloths have become collectible folk art, generating income for the Hmong while preserving their history.

Dia Cha's book uses text and storycloth photos to recount the Hmong's long and often harrowing struggle for self-determination. Ka and one of

Figure 2–1.

his aunts personalized that struggle by doing a show-and-tell for the class with one of their clan's storycloths. Students learned that thousands of Hmong were recruited and trained by the CIA for the U.S.'s so-called secret war in Laos. Several of Lenny's bookmarked Hmong sites confirmed the CIA-Hmong connection. Around 40,000 Hmong had been killed in the war and thousands more were murdered by the Pathet Lao or died in communist re-education camps after the U.S. withdrew from Southeast Asia in 1975.

The storycloth book was one of Lenny's after-lunch read-alouds and had followed *The People Could Fly* (Hamilton 1985), a classic African American liberation story of slavery days. Without any prompting from Lenny, students soon connected the two stories. Shirlon reflected on the Hmong's perilous journey from Laos, across the Mekong River, and into the relative safety of the Thai refugee camps, and in her biggest voice announced to the class that the Hmong "ran for freedom and got shot and killed just like we [the African Americans] did when there were slaves!"

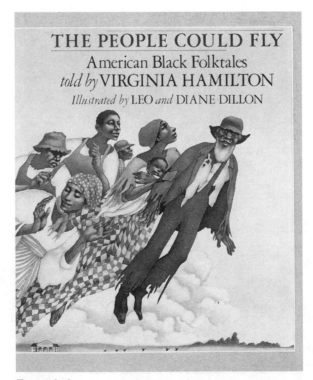

Figure 2–2.

Eugene, a Czech-American, told about his mom and dad narrowly escaping the Soviet tanks that ended the brief Prague Spring in 1968. Other stories bubbled up. Olivia and Gloria knew little about their families' trek from Mexico to the U.S., but thought the border crossing was "probably scary like the Hmong trying to get to the camps." Danny was missing even more details. He thought the trip "somebody in his family" made "a long time ago" from "someplace in the South, maybe Georgia, and up to Ohio" was really hard. Other kids drew a complete blank when Lenny asked them if they would like to share a little of their own story. Kids knew their heritage—Mexican, El Salvadoran, African, Irish, Swiss-Polish—but not their immigrant or in-country migration story. OK, thought Lenny, instant Social Studies Project. During the next week, kids researched their stories on the homefront, on the phone, on the Web, in library reference books, and wherever else the fact hunt took them.

The gathered facts were now going into six-panel storyboards as sequenced pictures. Kids were working in pairs with Emilio modeling and clarifying the storyboard process for Ka. Students would later use the storyboards as road maps for telling their stories to the class and for converting the tales to narrative writing. Ultimately, the stories would be published as a class anthology and distributed to parents, school staff, the public library, and the local historical society.

Language Snags

Ka began his storyboard tale at Ban Vinai refugee camp and finished up with a picture of Fitzgerald School. In the second panel, Ka had drawn a man lying on the ground with blood spurting from his side. Incense burned on a nearby altar. The man standing over him was dressed in a veil and finger bells, and must be a Hmong shaman, thought Lenny, if his online research information was correct.

The next day, with the storyboards completed, Ka and Emilio sat with Lenny and shared their tales. Ka's English was sometimes hard to understand. For example, Ka, like most Hmong speakers, had trouble with single consonants and consonant clusters following a vowel at the end of words. Lenny labored to make sense of words like *walked*, *bush*, and *fourth*. He had learned about these and other pronunciation snags from an ESL teacher support page at the Ohio Literacy Resource Center website (2001) and from an old but still helpful *Handbook for Teaching Hmong-Speaking Students* (Bliatout et al. 1988), developed by the Southeast Asia Community Resource Center at Folsom Cordova Unified School District in California. Lenny noted and zeroed in on the errors without overtly calling attention to them. He modeled standard English pronunciation for Ka, but did so as a natural part of asking questions and making comments about the boy's story. Several of his questions and comments had to be repeated, Lenny realized, because of Ka's difficulty hearing certain English phonemes that either did not exist in Hmong or had no close equivalent—sounds like the /g/ in *gone*, the /r/ in *run*, and the /w/ in *window*.

Later, Ka worked on a written version of his story and took it through three editing sessions, two with Lenny and one with Emilio. Both teacher and peer editor tagged several problem spots, though by no means all of them. Because Hmong lacked pronoun case and gender, Ka sometimes used *he* for *him* or *it* for *she*. He often left out subject pronouns altogether. His adjectives sometimes followed the noun, and many past tense verbs in the first draft were written in the present. Any one of the errors might hinder reader comprehension; collectively, Lenny knew they could kill it. But, again, he also knew the errors were typical of Hmong English language learners. Lots of errors went with the territory and Ka needed time to clean them up.

And Lenny needed time to learn more about the Hmong, especially the Hmong in America, a point driven home a few weeks after the family history story projects were completed. One of Ka's uncles called to explain that his nephew was sick and would miss school another two days. Lenny had read that the Hmong were animists and believed sickness was often caused by evil spirits who lured the soul from the body. Getting well sometimes required an animal sacrifice and a healing session with a shaman who found and returned the runaway soul. Lenny wished the boy well and then asked about the nature and course of Ka's illness, fully expecting the evil spirit, animal sacrifice, and shaman scenario. "Strep throat," answered the uncle, "but we went to the hospital and got antibiotics."

Reflections

Outside and Inside Stories

I thought of Lenny a few weeks ago when a teacher in a workshop asked a question related to one of her "Spanish" kids. The question dealt with the girl's "emotional turnoff" to English reading. Before fielding the question, I fished for more information. Was the girl newly arrived from Mexico?

Second- or third-generation Chicano? City- or country-raised Guatemalan? It was always possible that the girl was Spanish and hailed from Madrid or Sevilla, but unlikely given the district's—and the country's—demographics. Odds were far better that the teacher was using *Spanish* as a general term for any child who spoke Spanish as a first language. Answering the question required good background data, and good descriptors, and *Spanish* fell short by a mile.

The woman hesitated a moment, then admitted she wasn't sure about the girl's heritage. Mexican, she guessed. Another teacher wondered aloud how long the girl had been in class. "About four months," answered the woman, then added that she had just never gotten around to asking the girl where she was from. I bit my tongue, and I'm sure many others in the workshop did the same. Four months, and the woman was still clueless about the child's background. I knew Lenny would have had the descriptors and the background specifics all of us in the workshop needed to brainstorm answers to the woman's question. Lenny, as he did with Ka, would have taken the time to get the girl's *outside* story.

The outside story unfolds away from school and is built from a thousand and one experiences hooked to home, home country, and new country factors, including values, attitudes, worldview, family dynamics, communication style, language status, and political climate. Lenny understood that knowing Ka's outside story was as important as knowing his *inside* story, the story the boy was making from his new fifth-grade classroom experiences. Elements of the two stories intermingled, influenced one another, and made the *big* story—Ka's life in all its complexity (Figure 2–3).

Lenny pursued Ka's outside story for three basic reasons: respect, curiosity, and instruction. First, Lenny wanted Ka to feel like a valued new addition to the classroom community. As he visited with the boy about his experiences in Laos, Thailand, and the U.S., posed questions, shared his own understandings of Hmong culture, introduced Hmong books into the classroom, and gave the boy time to tell his story via storycloth and storyboard, the signal to Ka was loud and clear: I respect your background, your home culture, your language, you. Lenny sent the same respect signal to all his students by formally setting aside school time to hear everybody's outside story. Second, Lenny needed to satisfy his own curiosity about the Hmong. Teachers are inquisitive creatures, the sad-sack woman in the "Spanish" example above the exception to the rule. Most, like Lenny, want to know because most of us find knowing inherently fun and satisfying. Third, the knowledge and insights Lenny gained as he pieced together the

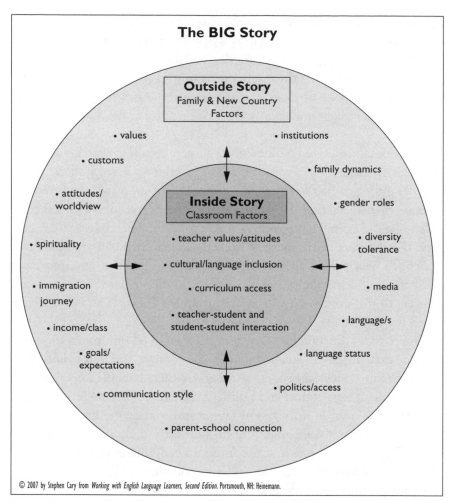

The BIG Story

Outside Story
Family & New Country
Factors

- values
- customs
- attitudes/worldview
- spirituality
- immigration journey
- income/class
- goals/expectations
- communication style
- parent-school connection

- institutions
- family dynamics
- gender roles
- diversity tolerance
- media
- language/s
- language status
- politics/access

Inside Story
Classroom Factors

- teacher values/attitudes
- cultural/language inclusion
- curriculum access
- teacher-student and student-student interaction

© 2007 by Stephen Cary from *Working with English Language Learners, Second Edition.* Portsmouth, NH: Heinemann.

Figure 2–3. A student's big story equals inside plus outside stories. Lines of influence run in both directions. Patterned after Cortés' Contextual Interaction Model (Cortés 1986).

outside story helped him modify the learning environment and improve instruction for Ka. For example, Lenny never demanded that Ka volunteer information or look him in the eye; he had learned that many Hmong children, like children from a number of Southeast Asian groups, defer to the teacher and avoid eye contact as a sign of respect. Misreading Ka's quietness and lack of eye contact as learner apathy, inattention, or defiance—then forcing talk and eye contact—may have had disastrous consequences for the teacher-student relationship and for Ka's learning.

Knowing the basics of how Hmong and English differed in sound, word, and sentence construction enabled Lenny to anticipate many of Ka's English language difficulties. He learned where and under what conditions Ka might have trouble understanding or producing English, and could modify instruction accordingly—with more modeling or with the strategically placed object, visual, synonym, paraphrase, or summary. Lenny's online ministudies in Hmong gave him a sense of the daunting task Ka faced as he moved into English. Errors would be plentiful, but natural. Ka's struggle with English comprehension and production implied no problem with learning, no disability. Nor would all errors be instances of negative transfer, with the first language getting in the way of the second. Most errors after the beginning stage of L2 acquisition would simply be developmental—errors that English learners typically make regardless of first language background (Odlin 2003; Brown 2007). The boy needed time, an engaging curriculum, and a comfortable environment to learn English. Lenny knew he would need the same things to grab a firm hold of Hmong.

Puzzle Pieces

Every new student is a puzzle, but the biggest puzzles are often those kids whose cultural backgrounds differ dramatically from our own. With Ka, Lenny quickly realized how many puzzle pieces he was missing. Ka's classmates were missing even more. Learning about the new boy and the Hmong required a multiresource approach. Relying on a single resource or even a couple different resources would have provided only a small part of Ka's outside story. Lenny needed the enrollment form, library reference books, trade books, websites, Hmong language lessons, a public librarian, teacher material from the State Department of Education, extended family members, and the in-class family history activities to solve the Ka puzzle.

And he needed Emilio. A peer buddy like this kid is worth his or her weight in gold, but even less skilled peer buddies can help us learn about new students. Cultural differences notwithstanding, peers share a common ground of needs and interests. That built-in connection can help new students open up and spin more of their outside story and spin it sooner than they normally would without the peer. Lenny was convinced, in fact, that the richness of autobiographical detail in Ka's storyboarded tale came in large part from Emilio's "good offices"—his friendly questions, his help with making English understandable, and his caring. A bilingual peer buddy, of course, would have allowed Ka to use Hmong for periodic content learning and more detailed background data sharing, but bilingual peer buddies are often unavailable. Lenny was fortunate to have Emilio as a backup; we should all be so lucky.

And yet, even with Emilio and a multiresource approach, Lenny never got all the information he wanted or needed on his new student's cultural background, never fully solved the Ka puzzle. Learning about a new culture takes time—and some caution. Pitfalls abound. Relying too heavily on the student for background data, for example, places a child in an uncomfortable and wholly unrealistic position, as teacher-anointed representative of "X" culture. No student can—or should have to—speak for all Hmong or all African Americans or all folks from St. Joe, Mo. Ka needed to tell *his* story, not the Hmong story. And, too, cultural information provided by a single student might be sketchy or inaccurate. There is also a danger in reading too much into group membership. Ka's Hmong heritage determined much about how he saw the world and navigated through it, but could not account for and would never account for all aspects of his identity.

Lenny avoided most of the cultural learning pitfalls, but not all of them. It was an easy tumble into the "concrete culture trap"—believing that home country culture somehow remains frozen and unchanged when transplanted to the new country. The antibiotics comment from Ka's uncle was a wake-up call, Lenny told me. He had forgotten, in his enthusiasm for learning traditional Hmong beliefs, that beliefs can shift in the face of new beliefs that confront the immigrant family on all sides. There is a continuum of acculturation for the Hmong, as for every group coming into the country. Hmong families, and individuals within those families, are at different points on the continuum depending on their experiences and time in the U.S. Ka's uncle had been in California for a number of years and had modified his belief system to accommodate a Western view of illness and healing.

I am always gentle with any teacher like Lenny who falls into the concrete culture trap, since I fall into the same trap myself like clockwork. Spanish is my (still developing!) second language and I jump on any chance to use and improve it. I continue to try out my Spanish with people who do not speak one word of Spanish, but seem like they should. These are usually extended family members of Spanish-speaking Latino friends, who have either lost their Spanish through the years or were robbed of the opportunity to ever develop it. I should know better after all this time, but I still stumble into the trap and chatter away in Spanish for a moment when first introduced. Some people never learn.

Discussion and Application

Discussion

1. Reflect on the linguistic diversity of your school and district. Are you working in a mostly bilingual environment where students speak English and/or another primary language? Or in a multilingual environment with students speaking a variety of first languages? If multilingual, how many different languages and dialects are spoken within the student and parent population? Do one or two languages predominate in terms of number of speakers? How many languages are "pocket" languages, spoken by only a small handful of students?

2. On a scale of one to five, how would you rate yourself on cultural knowledge regarding each of the non-English-speaking groups you work with? One means little knowledge of a group's history, values, customs, beliefs, and language; five means you could give a workshop to colleagues on the target group.

3. What activities, strategies, and resources are you currently using to get a student's outside story? What's giving you useful information? What's not? How are you using outside story information to inform and modify what you teach and how you teach it?

Application

1. Work as an ethnographer with students to map the cultural and linguistic landscape of your classroom. Specifics are essential. Knowing that a third of your students are native Spanish speakers, for example, is only a start. Spanish speakers might be from twenty or more different countries, including the U.S. Gather data on:

- primary languages and dialects
- home countries
- city vs. rural background
- L1 and L2 oral proficiency levels
- L1 and L2 literacy levels
- partial versus proficient (balanced) bilinguals
- multilingual students
- languages spoken at home (or per family history)

As Lenny discovered, time in the U.S. is critical to understanding where English language learners and their families are on the acculturation continuum. Include the number of students in the U.S. zero to six months, six months to a year, one to two years, two to three years, three to four years, four or more years.

2. Choose a cultural group you'd like to know more about. Base the choice on a group you're working with now or likely to work with soon. Take multiple source routes to expand your knowledge, using as many of the following resources as possible:

- teacher colleagues
- students and parents
- community liaisons
- community cultural centers
- books
- websites
- multicultural literature
- documentary and narrative films

Keep notes. Focus on practical information, those "got-to-know" items that will help you work more effectively with students and parents from the target cultural background. For example, what are the basic DOs and DON'Ts in social interaction? What should you say and do (verbal and nonverbal behavior) to ensure smooth and respectful communication? What should you avoid? What are the potential conflict points between school and group members related to values and practices? Also, be sure to zero in on the similarities and differences between students' first language and English regarding phonology (sounds), morphology (word structure), and syntax (sentence structure).

3. Consider the information you gathered above. For example, your language investigations may have revealed that:

- Verbs in Mandarin are "tenseless," relying on context and the inclusion of time words to indicate the "when" of an action or event.
- Vietnamese, like English, builds sentences using an S-V-O (subject-verb-object) pattern; Hopi, Japanese, and Korean use S-O-V (subject-object-verb).
- Heated oral debate and argumentative writing encouraged in the Western tradition may conflict with "the noncoercive style of the Navajo" (Dye 2002).

- Arabic speakers typically add a short vowel sound to three-segment initial consonant clusters (*i*string or *si*tring for string).
- Spanish generally flips the adjective-noun order and is heavily inflected, with verbs signaling time, person, and number.

All interesting facts, but let's move beyond academic exercise. Take what you've learned and use it to inform and modify a specific aspect of your curriculum, instruction, and assessment.

3

How do I make my spoken language more understandable?

The Classroom Story

Stone Fox

Stone Fox (Gardiner 1980) is a must do, thought Jeff, in between sips of coffee. He sat at the kitchen table, opened his plan book, and jotted down the title. Saturday morning planning was the rule. There would be no girlfriend, no movie, no free time fun of any sort till next school week was mapped out. *Stone Fox* was a favorite. It was on the district's core lit list, but Jeff would read *Stone Fox* to his fourth graders whether it made the list or not. The John Reynolds Gardiner book had it all: a fast-paced storyline, high adventure, superb writing, and characters you cared deeply about. Ten-year-old Willy's struggle to save the family farm in old Wyoming had been a winner with Jeff's students each year. Few tales

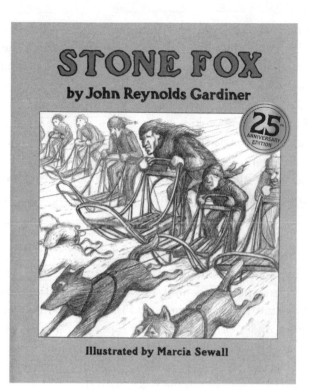

Figure 3–1.

could match the book's dogsled race ending for excitement, tragic surprise, and deliverance.

    Stone Fox was one of those books that got kids thinking, questioning,
and talking—even kids who normally held back. A good choice for the
first read-aloud. But Jeff worried how the book would fly this year, given
the change in class makeup. The Valley's population of immigrant families, especially families from Southeast Asia, was expanding rapidly, and
with it, Beiderbecke School's English language learner enrollment. Jeff's
ELL numbers had jumped from three to eleven in a single school year.
Five of the kids were from Laos, three from Cambodia, one from Vietnam,
and the other two from El Salvador. The students' ability to comprehend
spoken English ran from rock-bottom poor to near native level. Jeff knew
that a good half of his ELL kids would find the *Stone Fox* read-aloud a
tough listen. This book and all the read-alouds during the year would
need a lot of supplementing to make them understandable.

    Jeff poured himself another cup of coffee and began scribbling ideas
into his plan book. He would start *Stone Fox* on Wednesday. That would

give him a couple days to make or scrounge what he needed. Of course there was still a lot more planning and scrounging to do for other activities beyond the read-aloud. Jeff saw today's free time fading fast. Next Saturday's too. This was his fourth year teaching and he was still spending a large hunk of most weekends on work. He leaned back in his chair and looked out the kitchen window. Neighbor kids whizzed down the sidewalk on in-line skates. A family across the street packed their car with camping gear and headed for the mountains. For one very scary moment, Jeff thought teaching would never get easier—especially with second language students. This is it, he mused. All work and no dating. Good thing he liked the work.

Wine Box Sledding

After Monday's lesson on adding and subtracting decimals, Jeff asked the kids to put away their work and line up to go outside. Several kids reminded him that it was too early for PE. Jeff pulled two wooden wine boxes out from under his desk, grabbed rope from a cupboard, and told everybody that this wasn't PE. They were going to make dogsleds and race.

Jeff took a piece of chalk and drew start and finish lines on the blacktop, then asked two students to sit in the boxes with their feet dangling over the front ends. A classmate "dog" was hitched to each box with a rope around the waist and shoulders. On Jeff's mark, kids took turns dragging and racing each other the hundred yards across the playground. Back in class, the teacher told the kids he was thinking about reading a book Wednesday that had a big dogsled race in it. It was called *Stone Fox*. Good idea? Better than good, kids communicated with words and body language—great! Two students had already read the book and gave it a thumbs up. OK, thought Jeff; they're hooked.

During the free time reading block after lunch, four SLL kids with the lowest English skills sat at a table in the back of the room, put on headphones, and watched the first part of *Stone Fox* on video. They would watch a small section of the video each afternoon as a preview to the next day's read-aloud. The two Latino second language students, both good readers in their primary language, would read *Stone Fox* (Gardiner and Millet 1996) in Spanish.

Scene-Setter Visuals

Tuesday was jam-packed with California Gold Rush projects, book groups, and a graphing activity on the nutritional value of snack foods.

Jeff took twenty minutes in the busy schedule, however, to do a little more preparation work for tomorrow's reading of *Stone Fox*. Using pictures from the book copied onto overhead transparencies, Jeff asked the kids to tell what they saw and predict storyline elements. The book cover picture showed Stone Fox, the giant Shoshone mountain man who never lost a race, sledding neck and neck with little Willy and his devoted dog, Searchlight. Several students immediately related the picture to yesterday's wine box races.

As kids described the overheads and made predictions, Jeff would periodically take a word or phrase—*runners, wrinkled face, spot on the forehead, paw,* and *moccasin,* for example—and point to what it described in a picture. Most of the terms came from the students, but Jeff supplied a few, like *Samoyed, Shoshone, gaining on him,* and *swishing across the snow.* A three-minute clip from a travelogue video followed the book pictures. The clip spotlighted Wyoming in winter and was shown with the sound turned off. Jeff asked the kids to watch and see where Willy and Stone Fox would be racing in the book.

On Wednesday, several kids, including two of the ELL students, were asking for *Stone Fox* before the morning lunch count was done. A good sign, thought Jeff. After recess, it was time for the read-aloud. Kids were told to get comfortable; some slumped in their chairs, some rested a head on a table. A few plopped down into bean bag chairs in the carpeted library area. Kids could doodle if they wanted, toy with a puzzle, or do a small handcraft. There was one ironclad law: Don't make noise! Listen if you like the story; don't listen if you don't. But like it or not—don't make noise!

Jeff began with a short, three-sentence summary of Chapter One: "We're going to meet little Willy, his dog, and his Grandfather. We'll find out about how hard life is on their potato farm. And Grandfather gets sick and Doc Smith comes to help." Jeff read Chapter One, then summarized and read Chapter Two. At a couple points during each chapter, the teacher paused and asked two students, one ELL and one native English speaker, to help him walk through a piece of the story action.

Occasionally, Jeff paraphrased a section of text that he thought might be especially hard for English learner kids to understand. For example, in Chapter Two, when Doc Smith says to little Willy, "He'll be in good hands until the end comes," Jeff added, "Somebody who knows how to take care of old, sick people will watch Grandfather. And that person will take care of him until he dies." At other times, the teacher punctuated the reading with a brief display of one of Monday's transparencies, another picture, or an object—harmonica, silver dollar, potato, or bushel basket.

After each chapter, kids and teacher took a few minutes to offer reactions about what they liked and disliked about the reading, what surprised them, or what they found odd or confusing. During the discussions, Jeff noted that three of the ELL students, Seng, Tona, and Génaro, used terms plucked directly from the *Stone Fox* reading, and used them correctly. As the words surfaced, Jeff linked them whenever he could to movement, pictures, or objects.

Power Words

Near the end of the discussion, students were encouraged to grab a "power word." Everyone, including the teacher, kept a Personal Power Word List. These were terms that came from the read-alouds and other class activities. The criterion for picking power words was simple: pick words you really want to use, words that will make writing and speech more lively and communicative. There was also a Class Power Word List posted on one of the walls. Three words were added to the list each day, two by the students and one by the teacher. The list was color coded. Nouns were red, verbs were green, and adjectives were blue. Drawings or magazine picture cut-outs accompanied a few of the words. Kongphet, from Laos, chose a green word, *inspected*, for the list. Tona, a Cambodian student who had been in the U.S. about two years, chose *Searchlight*. Tona chuckled at the fact that with or without a capital letter, the word was still red. The terms on the class list were to give writing and talk a power boost as well, and also served as spelling words for the week. Three other wall lists were developed during the *Stone Fox* reading. One listed the names of all the kids' pets, living and dead (*Binky, Fua, Jeng*). Another provided alternative English words for *dog* (*hound, pooch, mutt, puppy*). The third offered a long list of breed names (*golden Lab, Siberian husky, Chihuahua, German shepherd*).

Jeff took another five days to complete the book, following the same three-step format of summary, reading, and discussion. Like the first two chapters, all subsequent chapters were supported with a variety of blocked action, visuals, and real objects. To follow the final thrills and spills of the dogsled competition, Jeff sketched out the race course on the large whiteboard in the front of the room. All the essential roads and landmarks were there—Main Street, North Road, the old church clock, the schoolhouse, the lake, and Grandfather's farm. As Jeff read, Maly, one of the Laotian students with very little second language, and Scott, a native English speaker, kept track of Willy's progress around the course with a pointer stick and a small plastic dog. Kids could hear the race and see it too.

Spin-Off Stories

Searchlight's sudden death at the end hit the class hard. Most kids in the room were shaken; several broke into tears. Jeff choked up and asked a student to read the last two pages. Twenty minutes of discussion followed. Kids shared feelings about Searchlight's death and talked a lot about how Stone Fox let Willy win the race. The death of the dog and Stone Fox's remarkable gesture of kindness generated a number of spin-off stories, some from the ELL students. Tona told how his dog almost died after it was hit by a car. Quay Binh described the death of a pig in Vietnam. Kongphet told about the many kindnesses of his grandmother and a favorite aunt. Many of the students wrote about Willy's loss of Searchlight in their book response journals. Some of the beginning-level English learner kids did picture-based entries and labeled their drawings with one or two words. Other students with more English did fewer drawings and wrote more text. Blas, one of the boys from El Salvador, wrote his entry in Spanish, then added a picture of Searchlight and Willy racing across a frozen lake and labeled it, *Wili and dog go*. Kham wrote *I cry* next to her drawing of Searchlight lying dead on the snow and *good Stone Fox is nice* below her picture of the big-hearted Shoshone.

After lunch, students volunteered to share journal entries. Jeff shared too. He wondered in his entry if he could ever get through *Stone Fox* without getting teary-eyed. The kids said he probably couldn't, and Jeff knew they were right.

Reflections

Building Understanding

Not all books that find their way on to a state- or district-mandated core literature list merit a yearly reading. A title that flies one year may crash the next, given a new set of kids with different backgrounds, interests, and academic needs. Some books on some lists, in fact, may not merit a reading any time. On the other hand, many books that teachers know would engage their kids may never make the official state or district list. These books are sometimes squeezed out of a read-aloud or book group slot by other "official" but far less stimulating titles.

Jeff was aware, however, that even with a good book-to-students match, any title read to nonnative speakers required some supports to aid comprehension. A business-as-usual read-aloud would not cut it. Given his number of beginning- to intermediate-level English learners, Jeff knew *Stone Fox* needed lots of scaffolding, lots of supports. A couple pictures and a paraphrase here and there would not fit the bill, especially for those students at square one English. A solid superstructure would have to be built around the book or kids would never be able to climb in and out of *Stone Fox* successfully.

Jeff saw the demographic writing on the classroom wall: Meeting the needs of a new student population required a change in instructional strategies and techniques. Some of Jeff's colleagues may never see the writing. Some will see it, but only with a large telescope. Others, who I occasionally stumble across on the consulting trail, see it plain as day, but still refuse to modify how they teach. I always try to slip in a diplomatic plug for early retirement with these last folks.

The wine box dogsledding was more than a terrific book hook. This was a foundation piece of scaffolding. Having a sense of what a sled is and how much strength and sustained energy output is needed to pull one were critical to understanding *Stone Fox*. Many kids in the room, not just ELL kids, Jeff felt, would have puzzled over the why of Searchlight's death without the blacktop sled races. Not every piece of literature, of course, lends itself to this type of whole-class physical involvement, but this one did and Jeff milked it for all it was worth.

For the English language learners, many of the key vocabulary terms—*dog team, contestants, hitched to the sled, picking up speed*—vital to following the *Stone Fox* story were introduced on the playground that very first day. Those front-loaded terms were then reinforced and others introduced the next day using overhead transparencies of the book pictures. The real advantage with the overheads is size: Images are big enough for everyone in the room to see, The actual drawings in *Stone Fox* are about four by five inches. Hundreds of trade books used for read-alouds have similarly sized pictures, which means kids sitting more than a few feet away from the teacher lose a lot of picture content. The loss is of little consequence to most native speakers who can grasp the story with or without the pictures. ELL kids, however, need the visuals and the many details they contain to help them make better sense of the read-aloud. For students with very low English proficiency, no picture often means no story.

Using Video

Moving pictures carry even more information. A video's images, speech, movement, and music provide a rich mix of meaning-building cues. Jeff knew that static visuals and objects alone would give his lowest-level second language learners only limited access to *Stone Fox*. A fuller understanding of the story required a wider road in, hence the daily video preview. Most teachers find their use of video increasing as their ELL numbers go up. Using video effectively, however, is no easy matter. Teachers must wrestle with a number of sticky issues. Four of the stickiest are acquisition, when-to-show, content variance, and fairness.

Acquisition   For starters, you've got to find the video and shlep it to class. That means a Netflix search (and wait) or a trip to the local Blockbuster, public library, or county office of education. Only a few searches and trips ever yield results; you'll soon discover that lots of great books you'd like to use for a read-aloud have no video parallel. Jeff told me he got lucky, but only after an hour's hunt at three video stores. Going online for an in-print check is an obvious time saver, though finding that the video exists won't guarantee local availability. Some schools use discretionary money to build a site-based stockpile of book videos, thereby cutting the "find-it" time to nearly nil. A few teachers spend big money on personal video collections. This usually means their significant other is working outside the world of education. Finally, many teachers I know who have worked with ELL kids for more than a couple years make heavy use of home-recorded shows like *Nova*, *Nature*, and National Geographic specials from PBS (Public Broadcasting Service). Other popular sources for programs include CNN (Cable News Network), local broadcast news and cable shows, and the Discovery and History channels. Teachers may use off-air recordings with students, but only in accordance with copyright and fair use guidelines. For a good overview of the guidelines, see www.wmich.edu/library/access/copyright.

When-to-Show   I always take a deep breath as the when-to-show issue surfaces in a workshop—sparks are sure to fly. Some teachers show the video after the read-aloud—and *only* after the read-aloud. Colleagues who present the video before, or even during the reading, like Jeff, are considered literature apostates who warrant a good flogging at a minimum.

The "Only After" folks mean well. They believe showing the video before all the reading is done degrades the book experience. And they have a good point: A book requires image making, with each reader and read-aloud listener constructing a slightly different set of images. Videos, on the other hand, provide one set of images for everyone. The fear is that video images will be stronger and more memorable than personally created book images. Only After teachers warn that a video shown before or during the reading can easily overpower the book and render it irrelevant. The fear of book degradation can be strong enough, in fact, to make some teachers avoid the use of book videos altogether—before, during, or after. The fatal flaw in the only after (or never) argument is that it assumes the reader/listener can "get the book"—understand the storyline and key concepts—via words only. Most native speakers can; unfortunately, most English language learners with low to moderate English can't. It's hard to degrade the "special book experience" that the Only After teachers talk about when the book isn't being experienced. Jeff's video previews each day provided his beginning-level ELL students with the means to "get" *Stone Fox*—not *Stone Fox* the read-aloud, much of which sailed over the heads of these kids—but *Stone Fox* the story, the core ideas.

Beyond basic access to the book, the video offered the four beginners a special advantage: an opportunity to build a little self-esteem. These students were the only kids in the room who saw the video, which differed in several important ways from the book, and thus the only kids who had the "knowledge goods" in class discussions that compared the two. Though the students often bridged through a bilingual classmate to get a point across, each was a giver. Video information turned the tables in the classroom; suddenly, it was native speakers, instead of ELL kids, who were the "information needy."

Content Variance   Book and video always differ, regardless of how faithful the video is to the original story. Rather than stumbling blocks to comprehension, the differences can make for better understanding of both book and video. The key, as Jeff discovered, is giving kids the time and the means to look at how the storyline is played out in the two media. Venn diagrams or a bubble map with some color coding are common tools for comparing a book and video. With the bubble map, for example, blue bubbles might indicate elements, such as a character, action, or relationship, that appear only in the book; red, those found only in the video; and green, elements found in both.

Fairness   Letting only four out of thirty kids watch the video can be a prescription for disaster. Reactions from the video-denied students may range from hurt feelings and shouts of "unfair!" to wild-eyed jealously. A teacher in one of my workshops told how videos reserved for her English language learners would sometimes disappear at the end of one day and reappear the next. Two of her native English speakers were taking them home to watch, then sneaking them back into class in the morning.

Here are two hints for avoiding or at least minimizing such problems. First, give all kids a crack at watching a special video. Individual and small group projects provide good opportunities. Second, talk to the kids about why ELL students might need to watch a video, and why they might need to watch more often than other students. In my coaching work with Jeff, I jotted down a comment he made to the ELL kids as they moved to the back of the class for the *Stone Fox* video, a comment that was purposefully loud enough to reach all students: "This is the way you're going to read the book." That made good sense to the native English speakers. The video wasn't a special privilege for the ELL kids; it was basic instructional material. In a sentence that would be used several times more, the teacher explained his methodology. Native speakers understood their classmates' need for the video because Jeff took the time to let them in on why he was doing what he was doing.

Instructional Grab Bag

Jeff saw the wine box sledding and the video as necessary but never as sufficient elements for making *Stone Fox* "doable" for his English language learners. Something else, a lot else in fact, was needed. He dipped into his instructional grab bag and pulled out an array of other strategies: primary language material, objects, visuals, text summarizing and paraphrasing, movement, action maps, power words, and student spin-off stories.

Jeff, in essence, played the percentages. With each additional strategy used, he made more of the book understandable for more kids. Video previews and Spanish reading, for example, built prior knowledge about dogsledding and Willy's relationship with his grandfather. That knowledge then made those story elements more intelligible when they surfaced in the read-aloud. Comprehension, however, was never 100 percent for any of the ELL students. In comparison to native speakers, second language kids missed more aspects of the storyline, nuances of character, and key concepts. Multiple strategies increase comprehension, but never guarantee it in full measure.

Postscript

Jeff was practically living at school when I began working with him as a coach. Not only was he not dating, he was barely making time to eat. Keeping school accessible for English language learners had become labor intensive in the extreme. We began exploring ways of making the job more manageable, of working smarter. Jeff's biggest time savers: having students gather and make many of the objects and visuals needed to contextualize activities; using the children's librarian at the local public library to locate and preview videos and video websites; recruiting university student volunteers to provide conceptual help in students' primary language; and exchanging content units and support materials with colleagues at the same grade level. Jeff learned that he couldn't do the job alone, and that he didn't have to. I'm happy to report that by the time our coaching sessions had ended, Jeff was dating again. And eating.

Discussion and Application

Discussion

1. Read-alouds are typically associated with the early grades, where they continue to be as common as sing-alongs, sock puppets, and turkey hand drawings. But you can find teachers reading to students throughout the grades: Eric Carle's (1996) *The Grouchy Ladybug* to the rugrat set; Alma Flor Ada's (1993) *My Name Is María Isabel* to third graders; Shel Silverstein poems to fifth graders; the latest Harry Potter book to seventh graders; Ray Bradbury short stories and slave narratives to high schoolers. And if we move beyond the traditional literature and social studies read-alouds, we discover a variety of "mini-reads," including school bulletins, news articles, notes, cards, letters, emails, math word problems, game rules, and test and activity directions.

Traditional read-alouds are powerful literacy builders. They can expand vocabulary, improve reading comprehension, and increase independent reading (Krashen 2004). And most students report they like the read-aloud experience (Wells 1985; Senechal et al. 1996), an important element in getting more students interested in reading. Beginning- to intermediate-level English learners, however, may receive few of the read-aloud benefits, if the reading is unsupported and therefore mostly incomprehensible.

Think about your own read-alouds, both traditional and mini-types. How comprehensible are they for your English learners? How are you determining that level of comprehension? Broaden the focus to include any oral instruction and interaction with students. What strategies and techniques are you using—besides offering the occasional definition or paraphrase—to contextualize your spoken language and boost comprehension?

2. Consider your use of video as a comprehension builder for read-alouds, thematic units, or direct instruction. What types of video are students watching? Film adaptations of novels? Biopics? Documentaries? Whole films or clips? How often are you using video? Daily? Weekly? Once in a blue moon? Are you using a mix of video sources: commercial DVDs, off-air recordings, web videos? Are most videos teacher-mediated or viewed independently by students? Finally, share your problems—and solutions—related to each of the chapter's sticky video issues: acquisition, when-to-show, content variance, and fairness.

3. Like many new teachers, Jeff felt the need to "go it alone," believing that highly competent and creative teachers can be and should be self-sufficient. The upshot was a life of round-the-clock schoolwork and not much else, a teacher destined for early burnout. Which of the following human resources are you using to make the job more manageable, to work smarter instead of longer and harder?

- teacher colleagues
- mentor teachers
- students (for gathering objects/visuals)
- cross-age tutors
- school and public librarians
- school-community liaisons
- parent and community volunteers
- international university student volunteers
- immigrant community center staff
- local university professors and graduate students

How often are you turning to the people who can typically help you the most: fellow teachers at your own school site? What stumbling blocks have you hit in attempting to collaborate with peers? What are some possible solutions for avoiding another stumble?

Application

1. Try an enhanced read-aloud. Do what you normally do to boost comprehension (for example, a preliminary picture walk), but add one or two strategies from Jeff's big bag of read-aloud tricks—video preview, story action walk-throughs, objects, power words, page/paragraph summarizing, paraphrases, picture-based book responses, primary language support material, or student spin-off stories. Decide how you'll determine whether the additional strategies increased comprehension. Possible indicators might include more students:

- attending to the reading
- able to retell the story
- providing accurate answers to comprehension checks
- telling relevant spin-off stories
- using key story vocabulary and structures in response journals (Figure 3–2).

Figure 3–2. Journal response to teacher-told story. Text reads: "I play with my dog. I can run with my dog and I love my dog." Dog's name is Lucky. Grade 3 ELL, early intermediate, Dover School, San Pablo, California. Teacher: Cheryl Namkung.

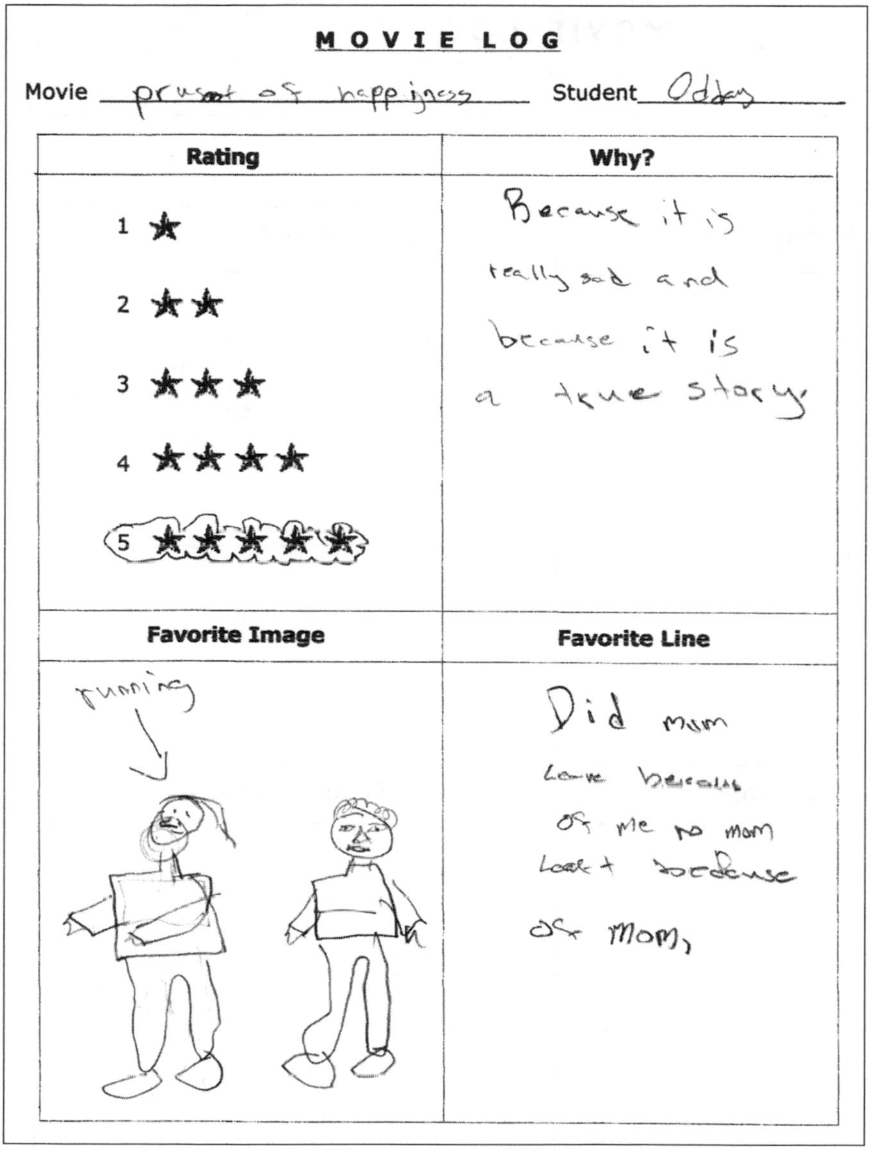

M O V I E L O G

Movie prusut of happiness   Student Oddey

Rating	Why?
1 ★ 2 ★★ 3 ★★★ 4 ★★★★ ⑤ ★★★★★	Because it is really sad and because it is a true story
Favorite Image	**Favorite Line**
running 	Did mum leave because of me no mom look because of mom,

Figure 3–3.   *Movie log based on out-of-class viewing. Film:* The Pursuit of Happyness. *Text reads: "Because it is really sad and because it is a true story. Did Mom leave because of me? No, Mom left because of Mom." Grade 6 ELL, early intermediate/intermediate, Westlake School, Daly City, California. Teacher: Beverly Williams*

MOVIE LOG

Movie_____   Student _____

Rating	Why?
1. ☆	
2. ☆ ☆	
3. ☆ ☆ ☆	
4. ☆ ☆ ☆ ☆	
5. ☆ ☆ ☆ ☆ ☆	
Favorite Image	**Favorite Line**

Figure 3–4.

2. Use video in a new way or for a new purpose. Some possibilities:

- If you're in the only-after-the-book camp, show the video as a comprension builder before or during the next read-aloud.
- If you primarily use video as a reward—"Finish that math and we'll watch ten minutes of *The Iron Giant!*"—make video and video-based activities an integral part of your next instructional unit.
- If you believe a video can't possibly be profitable unless it's patently— and oppressively!—"educational," try something a little lighter and a lot more fun and engaging. Example: Using Road Runner cartoons, which are constructed with a strict set of rules, to teach the math/ science concept of necessary and sufficient conditions.
- If you believe a video should always be watched in perfect silence, do a "watch and talk." Students sit in pairs or small groups and are free to comment and pose questions about the video as it runs. The activity can be a major generator of second language, especially in the early grades (Dragan 2005).
- If students are watching lots of movies at home and at the local multiplex, harness that interest. Have students keep movie logs (Figures 3–3 and 3–4), then periodically use the logs as a vehicle for discussing the latest in animated films and sci-fi blockbusters.

3. Break the "go-it-alone" syndrome. Approach a colleague and suggest a collaboration on your next unit. Plan together and share the work of gathering and creating the items you'll need to contextualize the unit's key concepts and activities.

4

How do I get my reluctant speakers to speak English?

READER'S GUIDE

English Language Learner Issue: Increasing second language speaking

Key Ideas
- Increase time and opportunities for meaningful talk
- Reduce teacher talk
- Incorporate students' personal interests
- Provide emotional "safe ground" for language risk-taking
- Encourage English speaking while honoring students' first language

Content:	Music; soccer; drama
Grade:	2
Teacher Experience:	8 years
ELL Language(s):	Spanish
School:	K–5, urban

The Classroom Story

Holdouts

The dog padded into the classroom and sniffed. He quickly separated all the pertinent smells: The frogs were in the back, hamsters to the right, the teacher's lunch—turkey on whole wheat—was in a drawer in a desk up front, and all the second graders were in the middle. Mr. Nakano, or "the Dog Guy" as he was affectionately known at Hampton School, gave a gentle tug on the animal's thick, braided leash. Nico stopped and stood motionless for a moment, then swished his broad tail a few times and sat down.

He looked friendly, but this was the biggest dog any of Cathy Sobil's kids had ever seen, too big for them to get up and pet right away. Even

Josh and Oscar, who were almost constantly in motion, stayed in their desks. The Saint Bernard weighed close to two hundred pounds and was about the same height sitting as a second grader was standing. The Dog Guy stressed how gentle Nico was, but kids were not so sure. It looked like you were a goner if he sat on you and you could probably drown in his slobber.

Mr. Nakano, the husband of one of the Hampton teachers, popped into the K–2 classes about once a month with a new dog for a show-and-tell. He ran a part-time dog-walking service in town and wanted to "share the wealth." Few teachers minded the short, impromptu visits. Students loved seeing and learning about the different breeds. The Dog Guy was a walking encyclopedia of pooch facts and was also great with kids. A few students were invited to the front of the classroom for a quick pet, and then Mr. Nakano asked for questions. Hands waved wildly all around the classroom. Bernabe asked something in Spanish. The Dog Guy told the class his Spanish was a little rusty, so one of Cathy's bilingual students translated the question, "How much does Nico eat every day?" A barrage of other questions followed.

Over half the class (eleven kids) spoke Spanish as a first language. Of the eleven, three were almost as comfortable in English as Spanish. The remaining eight had tested out as LEP (Limited English Proficient) on the district's English language proficiency instrument, scoring at the beginning, early intermediate, or intermediate level. Cathy noted that nearly all the second language learners asked the Dog Guy a question about Nico, mostly in English. But Erica, Gustavo, and Ofelia held back.

Holding back in English across a wide range of activities had been the pattern for the three kids since the start of the year. They spoke a few words of English now and then, but only if directly encouraged by the teacher or a classmate. Cathy's other beginners were "on track" and progressing nicely in oral English. But here it was November and all three remained reluctant speakers, especially Ofelia. Even Nico, the "gentle giant," had been unable to provoke an English response from them. By the end of the school year, all would be using English, including "The Silent Ofelia" as Cathy had secretly dubbed her. Yet each would follow a different path into second language speaking.

Erica

While students completed book response journals, Cathy asked Erica to join her at the listening center and help unpack a box of CDs. Every week the center showcased a different genre of music. As each CD was unpacked, Cathy commented briefly on the cover art, hoping to spark some conversation with Erica. Erica took the selections—Cajun, rocka-billy, big band swing, Latin jazz, blues, baroque—and arranged them in two neat rows across the center's table. Teacher and student put on head-phones and gave each of the CDs a quick spin. Erica listened politely to the teacher's running commentary on every selection, offered a one- or two-word response to the occasional question, but generally remained quiet throughout. This isn't working, Cathy thought. She had seen Erica several times at the center, eyes closed and head back, mouthing words and humming along with Ray Charles, Chavela Vargas, or The Beach Boys. The girl obviously loved music and Cathy thought going through the CDs and letting her choose the week's selection might get her talking. But so far, nothing.

The box was nearly empty when Erica fished out a CD by Irish fiddler Martin Hayes. The cover was pleasant but did not seem particulary talk-inducing. Hayes stood alone, pensive, hugging his violin to his chest. Erica stared intently at the picture, then suddenly opened up. "I know, Teacher! I know violín!" She popped the case and slid the disk into the player. A smile spread ear to ear. Then more language: "In México, in Michoacán, and I do the violín! And Alejandro, my brother he play!" Over the next few weeks, music, and violin music in particular, became Erica's focal point for English speaking. She brought her violin to school and gave a miniconcert for the class with her fourth-grade brother. With Cathy's help, Erica prepared and practiced one or two sentences to say before play-ing each song. Her short introductions provided the name of the tune, the genre, tempo, and country of origin. She learned the English names for some parts of the violin—*tuning pegs, fingerboard, f-holes, soundpost*—and used those terms to answer classmates' questions after the concert.

Each Friday, students reviewed the week's CD selection, sometimes orally and sometimes in writing. After the success of her miniconcert, Erica began volunteering oral reviews almost weekly—whether the selec-tion contained a violin or not. Her reviews, brief at first, quickly expanded. By the beginning of December, Cathy estimated that Erica had doubled her English output; by the end of February, she had quadrupled it. She was still talking music, but also math, science, history, the works. Erica was now using English with the teacher, with her classmates, and with the Dog Guy, who for balance sake, rolled into Hampton the next month with a Chihuahua named Betty.

mini concert & show & tell w/ her violin

Gustavo

Gustavo's T-shirt said it all: I DON'T PLAY SOCCER . . . I LIVE IT! Cathy knew the boy would play soccer twenty-four hours a day if school and his parents would allow it. He was on two teams and spent most weekdays and nearly every weekend on a soccer field, either at school or at one of the regional parks. Maybe Gustavo's love for soccer, Cathy reasoned, was like Erica's violin music—a good and handy route to English speaking. In PE, she had the boy help teach the class a variety of soccer skills. Unfortunately, Gustavo used little English to explain the finer points of ball handling—trapping, dribbling, passing, heading, and shooting—in large part the teacher realized, because his demonstrations were so good, only minimal explanation was needed. Cathy went back to the drawing board.

In her daily pull-aside ELD (English Language Development) sessions, the teacher incorporated several soccer-related activities, one on Pele, the legendary Brazilian star whom she knew Gustavo idolized. She made sure the class library was stocked with a number of soccer magazines. She also had the kids describe clips from a soccer blooper video one day. Finally, Cathy had a parent volunteer tape a soccer story that Gustavo could listen to as he followed along in the book. The story had lots of pictures and used language slightly above the boy's present English level. Surely, Gustavo would want to speak with her—or the parent volunteer—about the book, which another student had labeled "super good." Gustavo talked about the book, but only a little, and only at Cathy's urging.

A month of playing to Gustavo's soccer interest had paid few dividends. Cathy detected a small increase in the amount of English the boy was speaking, but that may have been wishful thinking on her part, she admitted, after putting so much work into the sports activities. Gustavo still spoke Spanish almost exclusively with his Spanish-speaking classmates and used English only when he had to. Cathy eased off the soccer, but continued to "pull" the boy into English with ELD sessions and lots of interactive work with native speakers.

By the end of the year, Gustavo's English had taken flight. He now used as much English in class as Spanish. What had happened in the interim—what spurred English talk so effectively, Cathy believed—was friendship. Over winter break, Gustavo had become best buddies with Marty. Their families attended the same church and began socializing. Marty joined one of Gustavo's soccer teams. Sleepovers and dual-family barbecues and camping trips followed. In and out of school, the boys became inseparable. They spoke mostly English together, a terrific help for Gustavo's second language development. But to her delight, Cathy discovered language was running in both directions. Marty was starting to use some Spanish, not just with Gustavo, but with several other Spanish speakers in the class.

Ofelia

Ofelia was another kettle of kid fish, thought Cathy. Erica and Gustavo were reluctant to speak English; Ofelia was unwilling. Playing to what appeared to be a strong interest—science—proved of no help. The girl stayed tight-lipped in English with or without magnets, microscopes, or plant experiments. She readily responded in Spanish when Cathy used one of the bilingual students as a bridge, but rarely in English. Socially, Ofelia had isolated herself from half the class. She was as uncommunicative with her native English-speaking peers as she was with the teacher—not unfriendly, but retiring and painfully shy. Cathy began hooking Ofelia with Susana any time kids worked in pairs. Susana was congenial and low-key. She was also bilingual, a little more comfortable in English than Spanish. The pair chemistry was good, but not magic. After a month, Ofelia spoke more English with Susana than anyone else in the classroom, but that still meant at most only a few sentences a day. Based on Ofelia's responses in ELD sessions and other classroom activities, Cathy knew the girl's comprehension of oral English was good and getting better. And she was starting to write some in English.

But speaking progress was glacial. When Ofelia did use English, she worried about how she sounded and how she put words together. She often followed up an English utterance with, "Is OK, that word, Teacher?" or "This is good when I say . . . ?" The girl was scared to death of getting English wrong—in front of the teacher and in front of her classmates.

Given the girl's second language "fear-factor," Cathy never dreamed Ofelia would open up on stage. Cathy read daily to kids, right after lunch. Books the class found especially appealing got a second or third read, sometimes with students acting out the storyline in tandem with the teacher's reading. For the playacting, students went to the "costume closet," a large cabinet in the back of the room, and pulled out appropriate items. The closet was stuffed with a wondrous array of wigs, shoes, thrift store clothing, props, puppets, rubber animal noses, and masks. Kids took turns as actors and could change their nonspeaking part into a speaking one if they wanted and if they could make their words "help the reading." The speaking parts typically amplified the basic storyline or took it in new and unexpected directions, which both teacher and kids found exciting.

For *Lon Po Po: A Red-Riding Hood Story from China* by Ed Young (1989), Ofelia played one of the three sisters who are home alone when visited by a very hungry wolf pretending to be their Po Po—their grandmother. Dressed in a long black wig, Chinese print blouse, and hanging on to a rope and a basket the sisters use to outwit (and kill) the wolf at the end of the story, Ofelia suddenly interjected, "You are bad wolf!" Cathy immediately abandoned the text, took the cue, and ran with it. She turned to Charles who was playing the wolf and asked him, "OK, Wolf, what do you say to that?"

Ofelia argued back and forth with the wolf in English for no more than thirty seconds, and only that one time in the story, but it was a start, Cathy reminded herself. And there would be more plays. Lots of them.

Reflections

Car Show

Teaching would be a lot easier if all kids used the same car and the same road to get to their second language. If all students drove new Ferraris or old Ford clunkers we would know their traveling speed—fast or slow. And if they all took Highway Ten and never Highways One through Nine, we would know which part of the road map to highlight to help them along. But kids move into their second language at different speeds and in different ways. That fact makes teaching a lot more exciting—imagine a car show with a hundred different models and another with only one or two—but a lot tougher.

Cathy saw Erica, Gustavo, and Ofelia moving at a slower clip with English speaking when compared to most other second language learners. It looked like Erica and Gustavo were driving Ford Fairlanes, and Ofelia, maybe a Model T. Cathy felt all three needed a gentle push down the road. But what kind of push for each child?

In our coaching dialogues, Cathy and I reflected on two essentials for increasing second language speaking—time to talk and a reason to talk. Time to talk meant more than giving kids time to motor comfortably down the developmental highway. It also meant providing them time and plenty of opportunities to talk in the classroom. Cathy told me one of the first requests she made after coming to Hampton was for new furniture, exchanging individual student desks for round tables. The tables made it easier for students to work together, to speak together. Though students sometimes worked alone or as a whole class, most activities were collaborative in nature and done in pairs or small groups. Cathy's favoring of collaborative, constructivist work over teacher-driven, teacher-delivered learning produced a class where kids talked as much and often more than the teacher. More talk and its flip side, more listening, meant more time for students to acquire the raw materials of speech—sounds and words tied to appropriate meanings, structures, and settings. More talk gave kids something to talk WITH. But why talk, why pick up the raw material, use it, and extend it, if there wasn't something you wanted to really talk about?

A reason to talk meant choosing and structuring activities in ways that made talk meaningful, activities where students felt a need to talk, couldn't help but talk. This in turn required curriculum content that engaged kids and reflected personal interests. Cathy took time to find out what Erica, Gustavo, and Ofelia enjoyed in life—music, soccer, and science experiments—and then incorporated those interests as best she could into the program. Meaningful talk means less "compliance" talk, the sort of talk I sometimes see in traditional ELD sessions. In such sessions, students respond to a series of teacher prompts, for example: What color is the horse? Tell Alfredo where you live. Ask Abdul if he likes strawberry ice cream. What did the girls do yesterday? Students dutifully comply and fulfill each teacher request to speak, but do so with the fewest words possible, rarely volunteer information or pose questions, and are glassy-eyed and detached much of the time. May the God of Teacher Coaches forgive me, but whenever I have to sit through a "Zombie ELD" session like that I always pray for a fire drill—something, anything, to get me and the kids out of the classroom.

Cathy worked hard at providing Erica, Gustavo, and Ofelia opportunities for meaningful talk, in and out of the ELD sessions. Unfortunately, honoring and exploiting personal student interests cannot guarantee English speaking miracles. Music-related activities were key to Erica's speaking development. Soccer- and science-based activities for Gustavo and Ofelia, however, never paid off as Cathy anticipated. Kids have a remarkable way of turning on the second language tap when and where they want, regardless of teachers' carefully orchestrated attempts to get them to turn it on sometime and somewhere else. Gustavo's English poured out with a classmate rather than with the teacher. For whatever reason—both needing a confidant, the soccer connection, a match of temperaments—Gustavo and Marty clicked. Activities with his new buddy provided Gustavo with hours and hours of comprehensible input— understandable messages—fundamental to developing communicative competence in a second language (Krashen 1985a, 2003).

Seeing a student gain so much language away from school can be sobering for some teachers, especially when the teacher has put a ton of time and energy into "maximizing language acquisition in the classroom," to quote Cathy. Cathy's efforts complemented Gustavo's out-of-class learning, but could never have replaced it.

From Drills to Romance

In workshops and coaching sessions, I sometimes tell the Maricela story to reinforce the importance of outside, learn-with-a-friend language acquisition. Maricela was a young woman I went ga-ga for on my first trip to Mexico as a college kid about thirty-five years ago. I hit Mexico with enough Spanish to order a plate of enchiladas and that was about it. I had been a bomb-out case with the audiolingual method in high school Spanish. The method emphasized mimicry, rote memorization, pattern drills, and canned dialogues, and left me—and thousands of other students around the country—with little second language for real communication (Brown 2007). My first year in college Spanish was better, but not by much. We spent the majority of time listening to the instructor's elaborate grammar explanations and doing Spanish-English literature translations. There were occasional opportunities to use the second language for authentic conversation, but they were few and far between.

Maricela, on the other hand, provided me with all the authentic conversation I could have hoped for. I met her at a restaurant in Mexico City and for two months I lived and breathed Spanish with her—at dinners at her parents' house, at concerts, museums, markets, archaeological ruins, and on travels to San Miguel de Allende and Oaxaca. Within a few weeks, I was speaking Spanish—not perfect Spanish by a long shot, but Spanish that got my basic points across, something I had been unable to do after several years of formal school Spanish. My second language take-off was hardly mysterious. I had the two key items that Cathy always tried to put in place for her English language learners: time to speak (round-the-clock) and a real reason to speak (friendship, romance, and culture).

Some teachers and districts, rather than leave friendships and the sort of language learning that springs from them to chance, have formalized the process. Often called ESL Buddy Programs, the programs hook each new immigrant second language learner and family with an EO (English Only) student and family. New and established kids and families socialize and discuss the ins and outs of school. And as was the case with Gustavo and Marty, they often turn language acquisition into a two-way street.

Taming the Crow

Ofelia frequently comes to mind when I'm asked about attention to language form. She is a great example of the kid whose editing crow is a real squawker. The editing crow sits on the shoulder of lots of kids—and lots of adults too—and listens for language errors. Any error detected in pronunciation, comparative adjectives, or word order, for example, and he screams bloody murder. He is ever watchful, always on guard for the speaker's deviation from standard English form.

Sometimes we need to be squawked at, of course, need to pay close attention to language form. Imagine not monitoring your speaking for slang and double entendres when making a formal presentation at an education conference. Or imagine the student who never gives a second thought to verb forms, unconcerned that the use of *I go* for *I went* could get in the way of communication. Form clearly matters. And research suggests that form-focused instruction within communicative-based, student-centered programs can increase students' rate and level of L2 acquisition (Doughty 2003; Williams 2005). When used and listened to judiciously, a good editing crow can help our speaking and our writing be more effective. Unfortunately, kids like Ofelia who overedit, whose crow shrieks at the drop of a final consonant or a blown phoneme, are so focused on language form, so worried about making errors that they often speak as little as possible. We need to use and risk with language to grow with language. But not speaking has its advantages: We stay on emotionally safe ground. We make fewer mistakes, and fewer mistakes can mean less criticism and hence, less embarrassment.

Knowing exactly what constitutes safe ground for one child versus another is tricky. Cathy told me she was close to passing over Ofelia for a part in the *Lon Po Po* drama because of the girl's language shyness. She changed her mind at the last minute and invited her up on stage. Though Cathy and I were never sure, perhaps the read-aloud drama enabled Ofelia to stay safe while risking in her second language. The sister character— not Ofelia—could make all the English errors she wanted. Either that or the girl really hated wolves! Regardless, the drama activity provided a good little push down the speaking road.

Postscript

I run across fewer and fewer teachers these days who see a student's primary language as an impediment to learning, something that must be "rooted out" and crushed as soon as possible. But they exist. I met a middle school PE instructor a few months ago who assigns ten push-ups to any student he catches speaking a language other than English. The fellow told me he believed the policy was "equitable" because he doled out the same punishment to kids regardless of language used—Spanish, Cantonese, Farsi, Korean, Vietnamese, Navajo, what have you.

So, here's a tip of the hat to Cathy and all teachers who encourage English speaking, who give the gentle push when needed, but do so without ever denigrating students' first language or suggesting they give that language up in any way. Thanks! ¡Gracias!

Discussion and Application

Discussion

1. No student group is ever monolithic. Any group we might name— Kinders, special ed, gifted, at-risk teens, 11th graders who salsa dance— contains students with a range of interests, experiences, personalities, skills, and aptitudes. This helps explain why within our group of English beginners, some students talk from day one, others gradually open up over several months, and still others are so reluctant to speak we're not sure they'll ever start.

Think about your own group of English language beginners. How many charge-ahead-from-the-git-go speakers do you have? Gradually developing speakers? Reluctant or highly reluctant speakers? Set aside concerns about the accuracy of L2 talk for a moment, and reflect on the frequency and quantity of talk. How often and how much are your beginners using English? Are they using their second language across the curriculum? Initiating in English? Asking questions? Risking mistakes in

English? Volunteering comments or speaking only when prompted or questioned?

2. Some students go through a mostly silent phase of several weeks or even months at the start of their L2 journey. They may use memorized words, phrases, and sentences known as formulaic language (Wood 2002), but are generally "quiet as church mice" as one teacher described a couple of her new immigrant fourth graders to me. They soak up language, but don't produce a lot. Other students, depending on interest level and background, may use varying amounts of English in different academic settings—completely close-mouthed during a literature circle discussion, for example, and then nonstop talkative during a rock and mineral sorting.

Beyond our silent phase and situation-specific nontalkers, however, we may still have a few students, including some adults, who plateau out—at least in the classroom—at the beginning and early intermediate levels. They start and stay mostly silent. While their classmates move from formulaic "chunks" to full-fledged discourse, using longer and longer stretches of language for extended communication, our plateau students remain stuck at an earlier developmental level. These are our L2 minimalists, typically favoring holophrastic forms like, "Take!" over the lengthier and more communicative, "I want to take the hamster home this weekend!"

What specific activities and strategies are you using with your reluctant/plateau students to increase the frequency and quantity of L2 speaking? What's working? What's not?

3. Think about how your district identifies, assists, and monitors the L2 progress of its highly reluctant speakers. Are the procedures effective? Are human resources being used in an efficient way? Are some students falling through the cracks and not getting the help they need?

Application

1. Though far from a sure bet, as Cathy would quickly remind us, playing to student interests opens the L2 speaking door for many second language learners. But it's hard to play to those interests if we don't know what they are. One quick way to learn about what students like to do in and out of school is through a short interest inventory, either oral, drawn, or written. Inventories can be as simple as a short "Favorite Activities" list as in

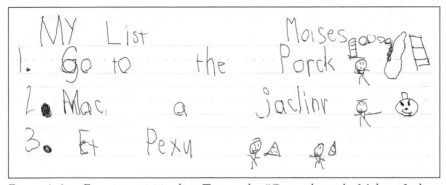

Figure 4–1. Favorite activities list. Text reads: "Go to the park. Make a Jack-o-lantern. Eat pizza." Grade 1 ELL, early intermediate, Martin School, South San Francisco, California. Teacher: Pat Dragan.

Figure 4–1, or more elaborate as in Figure 4–2 where students review a variety of categories and provide detailed information on their top three interests.

Administer an interest inventory to your students. If you're using a form similar to Figure 4–2, English beginners will need some translation help from a bilingual aide, peer buddy, cross-age tutor, or family member. Look over the results, zero in on an interest shared by several students, and then weave that interest into an activity or thematic unit.

2. Apart from incorporating student interests, consider the ways Cathy and other teachers increase L2 speaking, including:

- making content engaging
- favoring authentic talk over compliance talk
- emphasizing fluency over accuracy
- helping students know when and when *not* to listen to the "editing crow"
- having students share orally with a pair buddy or small group rather than the whole class
- having students talk through a puppet or role-play character
- configuring furniture for student-to-student talk
- paying attention to students' affective needs
- never forcing L2 production
- encouraging the use of second *and* first languages

Name _____ Date _____

Circle your <u>THREE</u> favorite interests.

Interest	Example
art	
collecting	
cooking	
games	
history	
model building	
movies	
music	
nature	
pets	
photography	
reading	
science	
sports	
TV/radio	
writing	
other	
other	

Figure 4–2.   Interest inventory. Students give specifics. For example, for collecting: U.S. and Mexican coins. Music: playing guitar with my sister. Reading: manga (Japanese comics) like Inu-Yasha *(1998).*

- doing more collaborative activities
- reducing teacher talk

Choose a new or infrequently used item from the list above and implement it in your classroom. Keep a daily journal noting any significant changes in the frequency and quantity of L2 use by your reluctant speakers. Include periodic verbatim samples to document student growth. If there's little or no change after a couple weeks, keep that item, but add another to the mix. Turning an L2 speaker from reluctant to enthusiastic takes time—and a variety of strategies!

3. If your school or district lacks an ESL buddy program, get one going! The programs come in all shapes and sizes to help newly arrived immigrant students and their families adjust to a new culture, learn English, and succeed in school. Investigate existing buddy programs in neighboring districts and beyond. Determine what program elements would work best for your given population, then put a small proposal together and formally submit your ideas to The Powers That Be. Hint: The program will have a much better chance getting off the ground—and being effective—if immigrant students and family members are involved at all stages of the planning, implementation, and assessment process.

5

How do I make a difficult textbook more readable?

READER'S GUIDE
English Language Learner Issue: Comprehensible academic text

Key Ideas
- Teach a variety of reading comprehension strategies
- Use text tours, graphic organizers, and main idea signposts
- Do think-out-loud modeling
- Offer multiple paths into the text
- Make text meaningful with personal stories

Content:	World studies; personal stories
Grade:	9–10
Teacher Experience:	24 years
ELL Language(s):	Vietnamese, Cantonese, Korean, Spanish, Thai, Japanese
School:	High school, urban

The Classroom Story

Text Tour

You could hear Karen laughing halfway down the hall, and that was with her classroom door closed. In class, the laugh could bowl you over; you either had to get out of the way or join in and roll down the laugh lane with her. Most people at Reinhardt School joined in and rolled. Students and colleagues alike marveled at how such a big laugh could come out of such a small woman. But there it was again, right in the middle of fourth period, SDAIE World Studies—explosive, operatic, and infectious. Karen had found something unintentionally funny in the social studies text and was roaring her head off. Karen's ninth and tenth graders caught the laugh bug and roared along. After a few seconds, everyone quieted down and returned to the book.

The teacher stood at the overhead projector showing a transparency of the opening page in a text chapter dealing with demographic diversity and social class in Latin America. Students' books were opened to the same page. Karen asked everyone to sit back at the small group tables and enjoy a text tour.

All the students were nonnative speakers. Most were at an early advanced level with good to excellent English oral skills. Only a few were at a lower, intermediate level. These less fluent students comprehended most of what was presented orally in class but had difficulty communicating the full range of their thoughts and opinions in English. Though the early advanced students were reading and writing in English, grade-level text was still a challenge. Intermediate students, who were still relatively new to English reading, found grade-level text mostly incomprehensible when they tackled it alone.

Karen popped on her tour guide cap, an old bus conductor's hat she had found in a Salvation Army thrift shop, and began the tour. As the official tour guide, her job was to lead students through the text chapter, pointing out the interesting and important sights along the way. Instructions for the tour were simple: "Watch what I look at on the page. Watch what I read first, second, and so on. Listen to what I think about when I start to read a piece of nonfiction like our textbook." She paused and quickly scanned the class to see if eyes and ears were with her. They were. "Listen to me think out loud."

"Let's hope I can still think," she added. "Sometimes my brain goes on vacation after third period." "Me, too, Teacher!" shouted Tomás, and Karen and class rolled down the laugh lane again. As the laughter dissipated, Karen pointed to two photos on the text transparency.

"I always look at the visuals, the pictures first—the photos or drawings or charts. They give me a lot of information. I don't need to start reading all the words yet." Karen covered up most of the text with sticky notes, then talked about what she saw in the photos.

"These photos also have captions to explain what's going on in the pictures." She invited the students to read the captions silently as she read them out loud, then said, "OK, it looks like this section of the book is going to talk about different kinds of people in Latin America. People who have different kinds of houses, different amounts of money. Let's see. . . ." Karen took a yellow pen and highlighted Social Class, which was written in large, bold letters at the top of the page.

"After the pictures, I usually look at the titles. And the biggest words on the page. And words that are boldfaced. *Social Class* is all three—a title, it's big, and it's bold—so I'm thinking these two words, *Social Class*, are really important—probably the topic, the subject, for this whole section of text. Good. The title supports or agrees with what the pictures are telling me. Now . . . I'm ready for more information, but I don't want to read the whole chapter yet. So I could. . . ."

"Read first sentence," Thao volunteered. Karen invited the young man to come to the overhead and read the first sentence in a few of the paragraphs. Thao shook his head. "Or read from your desk if you like," Karen quickly added. Thao read the first sentence in several paragraphs.

"Or we read part where is end and summary," Wing-yan offered, after Thao had finished.

"Good idea," agreed Karen. "Summary paragraphs and where the text says *in conclusion* can give us the important information in a few words. And those first sentences Thao read told me more about the topic—*social class*."

Karen paused and adjusted her hat. "OK, what did I learn?" she asked, hoping one of the students might jump in with an answer. No response. A little louder: "Hmm . . . What did I learn here?" Still nothing. She reminded herself that she had, after all, asked students to listen; this was another think-out-loud model, not a dialogue, at least not officially. All right, no pressure, no putting anybody on the spot. She would answer her own question.

"Well . . . I learned there's the lower, middle, and upper class. Three classes." As she named the classes, she dug into her purse and pulled out a dime, a five dollar bill, and finally a twenty. "The middle class is really growing fast. The lower class, the people with very little money . . . you can find them in big cities and out in the country too. A lot of the poor work on large farms that grow export crops, like. . . ."

Ki-ran raised a hand. "My uncles, one he is name Jiman. He worked on farming in Korea and he growed crops and my father work with him sometimes."

"Your uncle and your dad grew some crops?" Karen asked. "What did they grow?"

"They grow soybean," Ki-ran said, "and we didn't have crops sometime and was very hard. It is hard here in California but not hard with money like there."

Paphan offered a different view. "It's hard to get money in here too. We are poor in Thailand and we are poor in here. San Francisco is hard to buy rent and food and everything."

"Do you think that will change for you, Paphan?" asked Karen.

Paphan thought a moment. "I think we are going to middle class because of my school and I will get a good job and my brother and my sisters too."

"So good schools and good jobs help people change social class?"

"Yes!" answered Paphan, and several students nodded in agreement.

Celia was shaking her head at the back of the room and shouting, "No Teacher, no Teacher!"

Karen motioned Celia into the conversation. "But not if people is not like you and think you are bad and stupid like some people think of people who are not rich and are not speaking good English and look different and aren't white, like Latinos. Maybe you don't get jobs and then you don't get money!"

Karen cracked a tiny smile. Now we're cooking, she thought. The rest of the text tour could wait.

"So, even good schools and plenty of job opportunities are not enough to go from poor . . . to middle . . . to upper class?" She placed an extended hand on the floor and moved it up a couple feet as she called out each class division.

"Not enough!" declared Wing-yan. "Because hate can stop things, stop you from getting up high. You get beat, you feel beat and you stay down. You stay poor because of the hating you get!"

Yow, thought Karen, I've never seen this guy so wound up. Great.

She picked up the history book and waved it in the air. "I wonder if this chapter in our book talks about things like that—about hate and discrimination. Is there discrimination in Latin America, too, like here in the U.S.? Not liking people because of how they look or talk or how much money they have? Then not giving them opportunities because of all that?"

"In Mexico, yes," Celia answered, "there is hate sometimes for indios. I know that. You can see hate every days."

"Like in Japan, Koreans are discriminate sometime by Japanese people, the same," added Kumiko. "And I am feeling discriminate in the U.S. here sometime with my English. Two man laugh at me at Eastlake Mall I know for how I'm saying thing."

Other students shared personal experiences about real or perceived prejudice in the United States.

"It is immigrants who get the discriminating in this country," maintained Eduardo, "always the immigrants who are being hating and lose jobs. Like with Prop 227 [the 1998 California antibilingual education initiative]. People are not want us to speak Spanish, or Thao speak Vietnamese or anything, to be bilingual."

Jiman agreed. "The immigrants are always get put down, always just new people, just immigrants."

"Always just the immigrants? How about people like me?" Karen asked. Some heads nodded a yes but no one spoke.

Teacher Stories

Karen removed her tour guide cap and turned off the overhead. She walked to the back of the class and sat down in one of the vacant desks. Students swiveled in their seats and fixed their eyes on her. Karen bowed her head as if in prayer, then looked up at the ceiling for a moment. She cleared her throat and ran a hand slowly through her hair. The students waited for her to say something, to get on with the class. It looked like the text tour was over for good.

A few more seconds of silence, then Karen took a deep breath and told two short anecdotes about growing up African American and dirt poor in Georgia. One story spoke of Klan intimidation and violence, the other about job discrimination. Kids hung on her every word. Halfway through the first story, Karen suddenly stood and pantomimed a civil rights march and bloody confrontation with Klan demonstrators. Two student desks were overturned for a street barricade. Ki-ran's large white sweater served as an improvised hooded robe. Karen made a quick sketch of a German shepherd on the board, then grabbed a student's arm and feigned a police dog attack.

The students could hear the hurt and anger in Karen's voice, the same emotions that had been in some of their voices a few minutes earlier. When she finished, hands flew up all over the room. Some students had questions or wanted to make comments about the stories. Some, who had not shared before, shared now and related experiences from their home country or in the U.S. that reflected elements in Karen's autobiographical tales.

The following day, it was back to the text tour, with Karen and the students looking at more signposts to the chapter's main ideas—subheads, time lines, boxed sidebar text, and italicized and high-frequency vocabulary.

Again, each signpost located in the text was highlighted on an overhead transparency. Though the tour looked at each page in the chapter, only three text transparencies were needed to model most of the signposts. Like the day before, Karen thought out loud about which important idea or ideas each signpost pointed to. After about ten minutes, the tour ended and students began reading the text in pairs, a stronger reader usually working with a weaker reader. Karen encouraged two of the bilingual students to follow the English reading with a summary in their partner's primary language.

As they read, each pair took notes using a graphic organizer. The one-page organizer consisted of three large ovals where students recorded what they felt were the three key ideas in the chapter. In a circle below each oval, students wrote an interesting detail related to the key idea. At the bottom of the organizer, squares below the circles provided space for student questions regarding the key ideas and details—questions that were not answered in the text. Next to some of the shapes, students included small drawings to amplify a term or phrase they had written on their organizer.

Wall-to-Wall Grins

During the pair work, Karen circulated, posed questions, modeled the use of main idea signposts, discussed key ideas, and clarified difficult parts of the text when needed. Kazutoshi and Mari had misread the phrase *grinding stone* as *grinning stone* and had come to a dead stop in the text.

Karen encouraged them to push ahead in the reading or go back a little if they needed in order to see why *grinning stone* had to be something else—something that made more sense. "Look at what's being talked about near *grinning stone*," she suggested. Using the larger context, the pair quickly found clues—*turning it into dough* and *tortillas* that helped them make the repair and construct meaning.

"So the Guatemalans used a *grinding stone* and not a *grinning stone* to GRIND corn, right?" she asked the pair. "Yes," said Kazutoshi. "And they got awake three in the mornings to start grinding!" added Mari.

"Of course," Karen continued, her eyes beginning to twinkle, "you could use a GRINNING stone to grind corn if you wanted." The pair looked puzzled. Karen walked to her desk and returned with a large flat stone she used as a paperweight. She drew a big smiley face in pencil on it. Then, using large, exaggerated motions and sound effects, she pretended to grind an ear of corn she had drawn on a piece of scratch paper. Kazutoshi and Mari started giggling. Within a minute or two, Karen had shared the grinning stone joke with the entire class. Loud laughter filled the room and spilled out and down the hallway.

Karen knew what more loud laughter would likely trigger in the staff room over lunch. Mr. Tapley, another World Studies teacher who taught one door down from her and had the quietest classroom in the school and maybe the universe, would complain again about noise level and Karen's "ongoing history party." He would pretend to be kidding and yet Karen and everyone else on the staff knew Mr. Tapley didn't kid and was incapable of anything even remotely resembling humor.

Karen walked into the staff room at lunch that day wearing her bus conductor's hat and shouting, "Climb on board and sit any damn place you want!" Mr. Tapley winced and shook his head, but remained silent throughout his entire cup of instant noodles.

Reflections

Living with Textbooks

SDAIE is a real mouthful when fully spelled out: Specially Designed Academic Instruction in English. Often referred to as Sheltered Instruction, SDAIE focuses on core curriculum content and uses a rich variety of strategies and techniques, including objects, visuals, video, storyboarding, movement, role-plays, and collaborative learning to make that content understandable for ELL students (Krashen 1985b; Rosen and Sasser 1997; Echevarria et al. 2004). Along the way, and as a natural by-product of the approach's focus on accessible content, SDAIE expands students' English language skills. Mouthful or not, SDAIE has the goods for second language learners.

Authentic, grade-level textbooks play a part in nearly all SDAIE classes, including Karen's. Unlike some other teachers, though—SDAIE and mainstream both—Karen refused to marry the text. Her students used the state-approved World Studies text regularly, usually two or three times a week, but not exclusively. It was an important and valuable resource, supporting the curriculum but never driving it. And thank heavens, since few textbooks engage kids. Some texts are admittedly better than others, but that's a lot like saying some dentists are better than others; there's pain any way you go. Yet textbooks are a huge part of school, inescapable from the early grades through university doctoral programs.

Like many teachers, Karen was no fan of textbooks, but wanted to equip her students with the learning strategies they needed for success in high school and beyond. By necessity, that meant helping them deal effectively with textbooks—no easy matter.

For ELL students, even those with moderately strong literacy skills, few things are as daunting or as potentially demoralizing as an inch-and-a-half-thick textbook, designed for native English speakers, dense with print, bursting with facts and questions, and lousy with new vocabulary. Karen's text tours helped make the social studies book a lot less intimidating and a lot more user-friendly. With a mix of modeling and guided practice, students learned how to use idea signposts to locate the important information, the big ideas.

The modeling went beyond a simple naming of signposts and a reminder that these items can help a reader get to the heart of the text. Karen took the time to think out loud, to let students listen in on the internal dialogue proficient readers carry on with themselves as they attempt to make sense of what they read (Keene and Zimmermann 1997). Once a signpost was highlighted and defined, students heard the teacher questioning, hypothesizing, digging into the text for confirmation, and summarizing what she had found and what she was learning. Most students took the tour seriously and listened carefully, but not all. Those that failed to ride the tour bus this time, Karen hoped, would climb aboard at the next modeling.

One potential danger in modeling reading strategies, or any learning strategies, for that matter, is overmodeling. In our coaching dialogues, Karen discussed her ongoing struggle to "nail the modeling." Nail the modeling meant clear, carefully focused, out loud thinking. And for ELL students, especially, it meant modeling of a reasonable length. Fuzzy modeling or modeling that droned on and on for most of the period could be as overwhelming and as unfruitful as an inch and a half of you're-on-your-own, grade-level text. In my book, Karen nailed it.

As Karen's students became more comfortable using pictures, titles, subheads, and the other signposts, they became more comfortable with the text itself. Unmanageable text was now more manageable, more doable. Those generic signposts would help students deal more effectively with any textbook, not just their World Studies book. Main idea signposts alone, however, could not guarantee comprehension of the chapter. Other instructional strategies were needed if students were to build more meaning from the text. Pair work and primary language summaries ensured that the weaker English readers were on safe ground and could get quick help if they lost their way in the book. The graphic organizer provided the means to sort and rank ideas and to record facts and questions. The organizer was a note-taking and outlining tool that students later used as a road map for oral reports and longer pieces of expository writing.

Connecting with Personal Stories

Finally, it was Karen's use of storytelling and humor that carried the instructional day—that made the World Studies text a lot more understandable. She willingly let go of the text tour to make unscheduled stops for student stories and to spin two tales of her own.

Student stories helped activate prior knowledge, often referred to as schemata (Rumelhart 1980; Heffernan 2003)—information and beliefs about the world based on personal experiences. The stories also gave Karen some insight into how much students already knew about diversity and social class issues. Teacher stories, supported by a clever, skillful use of objects at hand, previewed terms and concepts coming up in the chapter text—and did so without any need for preplanning. A Klan story automatically targeted and illuminated the concepts of multiculturalism, racial politics, and the fight for social justice—themes coursing through the chapter. As they entered the text, students could hook new information in the reading to concepts and experiences they were already familiar with—like a snorkeler learning to scuba dive. The new sport required additional knowledge, to be sure, but you were still in the water and you were still swimming and dodging sharks.

Most importantly, the anecdotes provided a genuine reason to read. During the personal stories, Karen periodically circled back to the text, connecting elements in the stories to the material students would soon be reading. During the reading, students looked for reflections of their own stories—and Karen's—in the text. Personal stories had linked them emotionally to the World Studies text, which—and I'm being charitable—contained some of the driest and dullest prose you could ever put in the hands of young people.

The Ha-Ha Factor

What's in a laugh for English language learners? Karen and I agreed that the unqualified answer was: everything. Karen's freeflowing laughter and abundant joking created a relaxed, remarkably comfortable learning atmosphere. This was a classroom with high expectations, challenging content, and plenty of hard work, but a classroom where students knew they could lighten the load with a smile and a chuckle whenever needed.

The jokes and the laughs meant that World Studies content did not have to remain deadly serious day in and day out. And by logical extension, neither did the language used to speak, read, and write about that content. The freedom to laugh and make jokes translated into the freedom to risk with language, a prime requirement for language growth (Rubin and Thompson 1994). Karen's humor, more than anything else, was the real shelter in her sheltered instruction.

Liberated from the need to always be correct in English, Karen's high schoolers used English freely and frequently. They played with language, tested it out, made mistakes, listened and watched the teacher as she modeled standard forms within the context of World Studies activities, then grabbed those forms and cleaned up their English in order to communicate their ideas about class topics more effectively.

The surprising but sweet paradox: Giving students permission to get language wrong went a long way in helping them get it right.

Discussion and Application

Discussion

1. Think about the variety of academic texts you're asking your English language learners to read. In addition to standard, grade-level textbooks, this might include trade books, workbooks, test-prep materials, teacher-designed handouts, Web pages, newspapers, and magazines. How are students reading the assigned material? Alone? With a peer buddy? With a cross-age tutor? In small groups? In teacher-mediated sessions? Are you encouraging various ways of getting the reading done, or consistently favoring one approach over others?

2. Apart from the various reading configurations listed above, what strategies are you using to help your English language students make academic text more understandable and, therefore, more educationally profitable?

3. How would you characterize your use of grade-level textbooks?

- *Heavy.* Textbooks drive all planning, instruction, activities, and assessment.

- *Moderate*. Textbooks are used about half the time; a variety of SDAIE/sheltered materials (some with lower readability rates) are used the other half.
- *Light*. Textbooks are used sparingly, primarily as a supplement to SDAIE/sheltered materials and activities.

Consider the impact of your level of use on students' content learning and English acquisition. What are the pluses and minuses given a heavy use of grade-level textbooks? A light use?

Application

1. Consider the different strategies Karen used to make a difficult textbook more readable for her second language students, including:

- think-out-loud modeling
- highlighted text
- context clues
- objects, pantomime, movement
- tapping students' prior knowledge
- encouraging spin-off stories
- personal teacher stories
- signposts to the main ideas
- pair reading
- L1 summaries
- note-taking via graphic organizers and drawings (Figure 5–1)

Choose two or three new items from the list above and over the span of several weeks, implement them in your classroom. Based on informal and formal assessments (student comments and questions and text-based assignments or quizzes, for example), determine if the strategies are improving textbook comprehension. If you're seeing little or no improvement, don't lose heart! Keep those items, and add one or two more to your bag of instructional tricks. Helping students become more proficient at processing difficult L2 text takes time and the consistent application of a number of strategies.

2. Teacher modeling of the strategies proficient readers use to make meaning helps students become better readers (Chamot and O'Malley 1994; Keene and Zimmermann 1997). Not all modeling is effective, of course. Karen worked hard at keeping her modeling tightly focused, crystal clear, and just long enough to get the job done. Think about your own

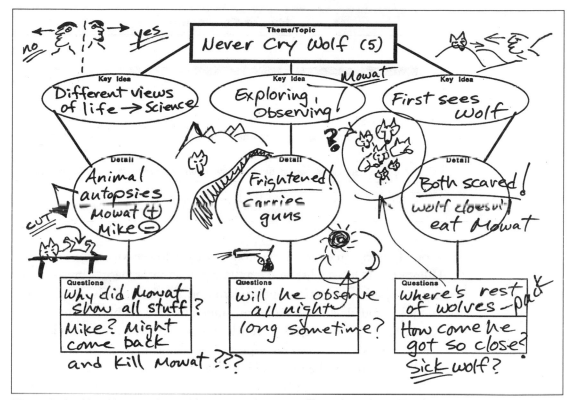

Figure 5–1. Graphic organizer with support drawings. Type: key ideas. Teacher-created overhead based on student input after pair reading, Never Cry Wolf (Mowat 2001/1963). Grade 10 ELLs, early advanced to advanced, sheltered literature/language arts class, San Francisco Bay Area high school, California. Teacher: author.

modeling of reading comprehension strategies in terms of focus, clarity, and length. Modify any element you find ineffective. Modifications might include:

- modeling fewer strategies at any one time
- using less or more sample text depending on the strategy target
- using more speech supports
- doing shorter but more frequent modeling sessions

3. Some students are highly reluctant to use L2 for fear of making mistakes and "looking bad" in front of teachers and peers. When serious and persistent, language anxiety can have negative effects on language acquisition (Oxford 1999; Horwitz 2001). Reducing students' fears and worries

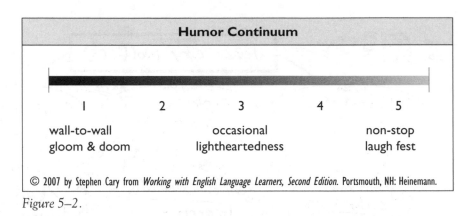

Figure 5–2.

about L2 usage requires a classroom with a low-anxiety environment. Humor can help establish and maintain that environment. Karen's attention to the ha-ha factor kept students on psychologically safe ground. Her jokes and playfulness served as a much needed counterbalance to the considerable—and sometimes overwhelming—challenge and stress learners face when asked to produce L2, process academic text, and master grade-level curriculum in their second language.

Reflect on the level of humor in your own classroom, then place an X where it falls on the Humor Continuum (Figure 5–2). If you've rated the classroom left of 3, consider boosting the ha-ha factor by:

- encouraging more student jokes and funny stories
- telling more jokes and funny stories yourself
- increasing the number of humorous read-aloud books
- sharing a daily cartoon or comic strip (see Cary [2004] for activity ideas)
- sharing a daily humorous video clip (from YouTube, for example)

Please remember that you don't need to be a stand-up comic or have jokes and laughter fill every moment of the day to score high on the humor continuum; you simply need to value humor, sanction it in the classroom, and make it an important instructional ally.

6

How do I help students improve their English writing?

READER'S GUIDE

English Language Learner Issue: Writing development

Key Ideas

- Have students write for real-world purposes
- Base writing content on student interests
- Understand the terrors and limitations of "compliance" writing
- Emphasize process over product, wholes over pieces
- Use a variety of writing supports (group composing, graphic organizers, drawing-based text, "skeletons")

Content:	City government; social action
Grade:	2–3
Teacher Experience:	7 years (2 as ESL teacher)
ELL Language(s):	Cantonese, Indonesian, Spanish, Russian
School:	K–5, urban

The Classroom Story

Mail Call

Yuen read the address on the envelope a second time just to make sure. Yep, this was for the principal, not for the kids in Mr. Ledesma's ESL room. She placed the envelope on top of the large *not ours* pile and fished another letter out of the mail basket. Not ours again. "I sure hope we get something today," Yuen thought to herself in Cantonese, and scanned the next piece for *Ledesma* and *ESL room*. Nope, not ours.

Yuen and the other second and third graders in Victor Ledesma's late morning group had written the mayor over three weeks ago. They all felt that was plenty of time for her to write back. But each day this week, one of the kids had gone to the office and carefully checked the mail and returned empty-handed. Victor had tried to prepare his early intermediate- and intermediate-level students for disappointment. Ms. Paolino, the mayor, was a really busy person, he explained, with a million and one tasks; she may not have the time to write back. There was another reason for a likely nonresponse, one Victor had not immediately shared with the class. In their dictated group letter, the kids had asked for something specific, something the mayor would find tricky if not impossible to deliver on: a traffic light. She might want to steer clear of McCrae Elementary and the potential political minefield.

McCrae sat in the heart of a large South Bay city. Cars and trucks whizzed by the school at all hours of the day and night, large numbers of them disregarding the posted yellow caution signs. Two parents had been struck pulling out of the parking lot, one last year and one this year. No one had been badly injured, but that was pure luck. Walking field trips to stores and a park in the neighborhood had shown students how dangerous traffic could be near McCrae. The car accidents underscored the danger. As kids talked about what they saw, heard, and felt on the neighborhood walks, what was good and bad, safe and unsafe about the local area, the traffic issue surfaced repeatedly. Victor mentioned that the mayor might not know how terrible the traffic is around the school. One of the students thought they should tell her. "In a letter?" the teacher asked. The letter idea sounded good to all eight kids.

Yuen scanned another four envelopes. Suddenly her eyes lit up. "ESL room! ESL room!" she shouted.

"Something good?" asked the school secretary sitting across from her.

"Yes!" replied Yuen. The envelope was big and official looking, with the city's seal and logo embossed in silver on the front. Something rattled inside when she gave it a little shake.

Yuen ran back to the ESL room with the long-awaited response. The mayor had sent each student a colorful city "booster" pin. She thanked the kids for their "informative" letter and promised to pass on their concerns regarding traffic to the Department of Public Works. Ms. Paolino closed by commending all the kids for their "active community involvement" and complimenting them on their "wonderful expertise in English."

Victor clarified some of the mayor's more difficult language. Then everybody read the letter a second time. Yeah, Okti was right; the mayor never mentioned the traffic light. Not even once. Could Ms. Paolino have missed their request? Kids and teacher didn't think so; they had underlined and boldfaced *traffic light*. They had carefully planned out what they wanted to say and emphasize. In fact, the whole letter had taken a lot more thought and a lot more time than Victor had anticipated.

Dear Ms. Mayor

At the start, the teacher recorded student ideas, "Things we want the mayor to know," on a moveable whiteboard. He drew a rectangle on the board with a postage stamp in the right corner and some squiggly address lines in the middle, and labeled it LETTER. Victor boiled each idea down to a few words and placed the words in circles around the rectangle. A single line connected each circle to the LETTER. After ten minutes of brainstorming, students had filled the board with points they wanted to make in their letter to the mayor, including: dangerous street; people speed; long time to cross; too many cars; signs not helping; someone will die; parents in accidents; noisy trucks. Beside a few circles, Victor drew pictures to help with comprehension of the bubbled text.

The teacher reminded the kids how busy the mayor was and how she might only have time to read a short letter. What were the three most important points they wanted to make? After a few more minutes of discussion, with Victor posing questions and explaining a word or phrase here and there, kids decided that the mayor needed to learn about the danger, the accidents, and the speeding cars. Circles with less important ideas were erased. Victor was ready to take the next step and compose the letter with the kids when Okti shouted out an idea.

"We need up thing and telling OK! you going in the street and the thing saying no no now not going!"

Victor wasn't sure what the lanky, big-voiced girl from Indonesia was trying to communicate, but Jaime got it. "Okti says a stop light."

Victor turned to Okti. "A stop light, Okti? A traffic light?" Okti gave a tentative nod. Victor pointed to the ceiling to indicate a traffic light above an intersection, then made some car engine sounds, and pantomimed a driver looking up at the light and braking to a full stop.

Before Victor finished his little drama, Okti yelled, "Yes! We need. We need for safe!"

The class agreed. Victor added a circle to the whiteboard and drew an outline of a traffic light inside. Okti came to the board and finished the light with large dots of red, yellow, and green. OK, thought Victor, we'll make four points in the letter instead of three.

The next day, Victor began with the circled ideas. Students had to decide on an order for making their points. What would be a good beginning? A strong ending? Kids decided that they would talk about the accidents first. That was serious stuff and would get the mayor's attention. Serguei went to the board and put a "1" by the accident circle. Speeding cars would be next, followed by something about how dangerous the situation was for everybody at the school. They would end the letter with the fourth point and what they wanted from the mayor: a traffic light.

Next, Victor drew a letter "skeleton" on the board with lined out areas for school address, mayor's address, salutation, body, and closing. Before turning to the kids for the opening sentence, he reminded everyone that they would be making lots of writing errors. That was natural in a second language—for everybody—especially at the beginning. To drive the point home, the teacher held up a four-sentence note he had written in Spanish and planned to send to the parents of a girl in his early morning group. His work had been checked by another teacher at McCrae who was bilingual. The note had at least a dozen errors circled in red. Victor waved the note above his head and proudly declared, "I'm getting better!" He laughed and the kids laughed with him.

Victor asked students if they wanted him to "fix up" the English as they went along. A letter without a lot of mistakes, he said, could get their ideas across better to the mayor. All agreed to the fix-ups. As a line was suggested, Victor rephrased it when necessary, making subjects and verbs agree, correcting tense and word-order problems, or offering an alternative word that might give the sentence more clarity or strength. What he never changed in a sentence was the student's basic message—unless the message dropped out of left field and distorted the key points kids had agreed on. Victor checked to make sure everyone understood the rephrased sentence, then added it to the letter skeleton.

Students continued through their four-point sequence, and the letter to Ms. Paolino took shape. By the end of the forty-five-minute session, kids had finished the letter and with Victor's guidance checked it for meaning, then for spelling, capitals, and punctuation.

The teacher typed it up and during the next session kids looked the letter over one last time. After a couple minor revisions, Victor asked the kids if the letter said what they wanted it to say. It did. The next day students popped the letter into a nearby mail box and waited for the mayor to write back and tell them when the traffic light would be installed.

More Letters, More Pins

Nearly a month had passed without a response. Now the mayor's letter had finally rolled in, with the buck passing to the Department of Public Works and with no word of the light. Victor gave the kids a sense of what Public Works was all about by walking them outside for a minute to watch a city work crew fill potholes a couple blocks from the school. Other crews from the department, he informed the students, handled jobs like traffic light installation.

The kids decided it was important to follow up with the department and check on their light. Maybe the mayor forgot to tell Public Works about the light just like she had forgotten about it in her letter. This time they would each write a letter because Victor had said that eight letters could be more convincing than one. Based on another suggestion from the teacher, students made sure the mayor knew they still wanted her to help them get a light. At the bottom left of each letter, students wrote: *cc: Mayor Paolino.*

Over the next four months, kids exchanged a series of letters and email with the Department of Public Works, the Police Department, and the Mayor's office. As students began their individual letters, Victor explained that each letter would look different from the rest. Some letters would be written mostly in pictures, some mostly in words, and some in a mix of the two. The look of a letter depended on how much English a student had "to play with." How much English students had to play with, however, could and did change quickly as they shaped and reshaped their letters in a series of teacher-guided steps.

Kids gathered the information they needed for the letters using a variety of resources, including newspapers, interviews with parents and students, picture dictionaries, phone books, demographic tables, city brochures, and a Chamber of Commerce–made video town tour, where, not too surprisingly, there wasn't a single speeding car in sight. Students brainstormed and mapped out letter content with Victor, labeled pictures, posed questions, traded reactions on various drafts, and struggled to make sense of letters they got back from city officials.

As students gained more English—and more confidence in their ability to write in English—syntax, spelling, punctuation, capitalization, and word usage improved. The letters, though still far from native English level, grew in length, complexity, and communicative punch. In short, student letters at the end of the "traffic light unit" said more, said it better, and said it more correctly than letters at the beginning. At regular junctures throughout the process, Victor and the kids squirreled away a number of drafts and copies of final letters in student portfolios. The work would help document for all concerned—from kids and teacher to parents, administrators, and state program reviewers—the type and degree of progress students had made in second language writing.

Early on, students discovered that getting a light would take some time. And some money: A basic, no-frills traffic light would cost the city about a hundred and twenty thousand dollars. The principal got wind of the project and gave his unqualified blessing. With the help of parents and teachers on the McCrae Site Council, Victor's students filled out a formal petition and submitted it to the city's Traffic Safety Committee. Student drawings of cars and trucks rushing recklessly past the school accompanied the petition.

The Traffic Safety Committee sat on the petition for a month, then sent the kids a polite thank-you and a big package of note pads, pencils, and refrigerator magnets with the city seal and logo stamped on everything. Plus some more pins. The committee would do a traffic count at McCrae and then carefully review the school's request within four to six months.

The upshot? The kids never got their light, but as Victor liked to remind everybody, they sure learned to write one terrific complaint letter.

Reflections

Writing for a Purpose

As teachers shop for ideas on how to help kids with writing, it makes sense to turn to the people who know the most about writing: real writers. By real writers, I mean more than the standard crew of journalists, novelists, playwrights, and poets. I mean my home insurance agent and my dog's vet, too. All of them write and all of them write for a purpose. Journalists, for example, aim to convey facts; poets, image and emotion. My home insurance agent aims to sell me another rider I could probably live without. And my vet aims for detailed medical records on Maggie, the Completely Spoiled Princess Pooch.

All of them write to be read, and so all the real writers have real readers, whether newspaper subscribers, poetry buffs, overly insured homeowners, or anxious pet parents. To get good writing—writing that has a chance of being read and understood—all the writers run their work through several think, write, and revise cycles. Finally, real writers never write in a vacuum. As the think, write, and revise cycles play out, writers get reaction and improvement hints from editors, faithful readers, friends, clients, and colleagues.

Victor looked at how real writers write, then used what he saw them doing as an instructional template to help ELL kids improve their writing. Like writers in the world outside school, his students wrote for a purpose: to get that traffic light! They had a large and ever-expanding flock of readers—the mayor, the police chief, cubicled bureaucrats, the principal, parents, teachers, and other students. His kids thought, wrote, and revised, over and over again, both as a group and as individual writers. And throughout the process, students could always turn to Victor or a classmate for a writing "fix-up." There was always someone there to help make the writing better—to repair an idiom, supply a capital letter or a comma, substitute a stronger adjective, or realign syntax—so the words would say what a student wanted and needed them to say.

Other supports, like group letter dictation, graphic organizers with drawings, pantomime, heavy rephrasing, and showing rather than simply telling what Public Works' crews did, helped make the content of the traffic light writing more understandable and therefore more doable for English language learners. Moreover, allowing individual letters to "look different" meant that each student, regardless of English language proficiency, could write a letter or send an email and play an active, integral part in the quest for a light.

Skills for Skills

This was Victor's second year as an ESL pull-out teacher and there was a dramatic difference, he told me, between year one and two in what kids wrote and how they wrote it. Like many teachers, Victor had turned to a write-for-real, process-based approach to writing (Kroll 2001; Graves 2003) after not getting the mileage he wanted out of a more traditional, skills-based program. The skills-based route made good sense at first. Nearly every teacher sending children to the ESL room had asked him— almost begged him—to work on English writing skills. Teachers rarely if ever spoke of a context for the skills—a poem, story, business letter, book report, science log—just skills. The principal asked for skills too, and gave him "the bible" for building his ESL program: a thick binder holding the district's ELD (English Language Development) Scope and Sequence and a copy of the state's proposed ELD Standards. In both documents, dozens upon dozens of skills were parted out per language proficiency level and neatly boxed under the areas of listening, speaking, reading, and writing. The state standards were particularly detailed, and were pigeon-holed within four grade divisions and five proficiency levels, two more levels than the district used: beginning, early intermediate, intermediate, early advanced, and advanced. Finally, many of the materials, like the writing workbooks ordered by the previous ESL teacher and inherited by Victor, reflected a sequenced skills orientation to teaching English language learners. Though Victor had taught for several years, he was new to pull-out programs and to the entire craft of teaching English as a Second Language. Skills, at least according to many of his colleagues and his boss, was the name of the game in ESL, and so Victor quite naturally started with skills.

Most of the activities and exercises in the hand-me-down writing workbooks taught and reinforced a specific skill—asking *who? where?* and *why?* questions, forming irregular past tense verbs, using adverbs of frequency. The purpose of the workbooks, according to the author's introductory notes, was to "reinforce oral lessons" and provide students with opportunities for "independent written work." What the books asked kids to do was to learn language piece by piece, with each piece, such as the possessive adjectives in the following example, isolated from the other pieces.

1. He picks up *his* toys.
2. I brush *my* teeth.
3. Graciela walks *her* dog.
4. Doug and Eddie sing *their* song.
5. We paint in *our* classroom.

Learning English like this was a lot like trying to learn to swing dance by taking a day to practice what the left foot does, then a day for the right, another for the left arm, then the right arm, the chest, and finally the head. Like a dancer in motion, language is an integrated and interdependent system. Though we pay attention to the individual pieces—lift that left foot higher! if you're a jitterbug; watch those prepositions! if you're an ESL student—each piece is learned best and, in fact, only makes sense as part of a working, meaningful whole (Goodman 1996; Freeman and Freeman 1998).

Victor marched the kids through the workbooks for a couple weeks, then, reaching a page on coordinating conjunctions, suddenly called it quits. The page asked students to use small picture cues and a written model to turn two sentences into one:

1. I eat an orange. Nick eats an apple.
   I eat an orange, *but* Nick eats an apple.
2. She buys a book. I buy a pencil.
   She buys a book, *but* I buy a pencil.
3. Lilly plays piano. We play guitar.
   Lilly plays piano, *but* we play guitar.

Victor wasn't sure who found this page and all the others like it in the books more painful—kids or teacher. He buried the workbooks on a bottom shelf in one of the cabinets in the back of the room and returned to the start line. After several failed attempts to get kids "writing with enthusiasm" using story starters—My Favorite Animal; My Favorite TV Show; A Description of My Best Friend; What I Like Best/Least About the U.S.—Victor turned to one of the district resource teachers for help.

The resource teacher supplied a newer set of ESL materials that Victor thought was a big improvement over the old workbooks and story starters. The set included high-interest stories and folktales from many different cultures, colorful posters, and sing-along books and CDs. Activities in the program integrated science, math, and social studies, and there were ample opportunities for writing throughout.

Though now part of a working whole—writing and responding to *why?* questions for the protagonist in a literature read-aloud or using irregular past tense verbs in a hamster observation log—student writing still felt a little forced from time to time. The moans and groans that had accompanied the workbook writing had stopped and students readily complied with the new materials' prompts to write, but no one was eager to write, no one was choosing to write on his or her own. And students were not writing a lot when they did write. Pieces were still short; kids wrote only as much as they had to write.

Letter War

Once the search for the Holy Grail, aka the hundred-and-twenty-thousand-dollar traffic light, was under way, kids never needed a prod to start writing or another to keep writing once they started. Instead, there were times during the "letter war" between the forces of good (clearly the kids!)

and the forces of evil (clearly the bureaucrats!) when Victor needed to ask students to *stop* writing so they could move on to other content-based activities.

Quantity and quality of writing increased in direct proportion to the genuine need to write. Kids wanted a traffic light, but couldn't get a light without writing a lot of letters and email. They quickly learned that their letters and email would go unread and therefore unheeded if they weren't readable and persuasive. Making them readable and persuasive meant kids needed a variety of writing skills, including:

- writing simple sentences about an event;
- creating cohesive paragraphs that develop a central idea;
- using correct subject-verb agreement;
- producing independent writing with consistent use of capitalization, punctuation, and correct spelling.

The basic message was about as plain as anything could be: No writing skills, no light.

Victor had intensified students' need to write as he modified his program, letting go of the workbooks and story starters and moving to more meaningful writing within a content-based, problem-solving approach. Victor, like so many teachers, found that student-centered writing and skill building were not mutually exclusive. Writing from genuine need, writing from the heart and taking that writing through a series of editing cycles, got you skills, skills—should anyone need the reassurance—that appear in any ESL scope and sequence or standards matrix worth its salt.

Unfortunately, an increase in writing skills was not enough to guarantee a new traffic light for McCrae Elementary. Victor described the kids as disappointed, but not crushed. They felt good about trying to do something positive for the school and good about how much they had learned about letter writing and city government. They had also learned an indispensable phrase in English for weathering the rigors of the American political system: win some, lose some.

Discussion and Application

Discussion

1. Think about a typical week's work of writing done by your English language learners. Consider *what* they write, *how* they write it, and *who* they write it for.

Are students doing more

- compliance or student-centered writing?
- single- or multiple-genre writing?
- single-purpose or multipurpose writing?
- independent or pair/group writing?
- single-mode (words only) or dual-mode (words + pictures) writing?
- in-school or out-of-school writing?

Does your writing program and instruction focus more on

- form or message?
- product or process?
- narrow or broad-based content?
- teacher or students/others as audience?
- single or multiple think, write, and revise cycles?

What aspects of the current *what, how,* and *who* need modifying to achieve a more balanced, more effective L2 writing program?

2. Some teachers, like Victor, help students build writing skills via a critical literacy approach (Freire 1970; Ada 1988; Wink 2000), which emphasizes text analysis, personal reflection, and social action to address local issues, injustices, and inequities. For example, Victor's students carefully scrutinized letters from city personnel (text analysis), thought about what the school community really needed to improve safety (personal reflection), and launched a sustained letter/email campaign to get the traffic light (social action). If you've used a critical literacy approach, briefly describe one or more social issues your students tackled. What were the effects of the approach and activities on students' L2 writing development?

3. Teachers, especially new teachers, often feel compelled to use state- or district-mandated reading/writing programs, even when the material is cumbersome, scripted to prevent teacher deviation, lacks solid research support, is disconnected from real-world language use, and bores students (and teachers!) to death (Garan 2002). Use it and you keep your job; don't use it and good luck paying the rent. Fortunately, there's a middle-ground position where you can stay employed and still do right by students: Use the mandated text, workbook, or kit, but heavily supplement it with other, more effective materials and activities.

If you're in a "Use it or die!" position, as one teacher I recently coached called it, how are you coping with the material mandate? Tears? Towing the line? Supplementing? Joining with other disheartened teachers to fight the mandates at local, state, and federal levels?

Application

1. Consider the many strategies Victor used to support and develop his students' L2 writing during the traffic light quest:

- teacher-led group writing (Figure 6–1)
- multiple think, write, and revise cycles
- graphic organizers with drawings (Figure 6–2)

Figure 6–1. School newspaper. Teacher-facilitated student group writing. Student photographer. Grade 1 ELLs, beginning to early advanced, Martin School, South San Francisco, California. Teacher: Pat Dragan.

Figure 6–2. Graphic organizer with support drawings. Type: basic bubble map. Teacher-created at overhead based on student input after teacher-told tall tale, "Peanut Butter Everywhere!" Grade 4–5 ELLs, early intermediate to early advanced, Hoover School, Redwood City, California. Teacher: author.

- letter skeletons
- differentiated writing (words or words + pictures)
- pantomime, movement (Figure 6–3)
- prioritizing/sequencing student ideas
- rephrasing (recasting)
- key vocabulary
- ongoing reminders that writing mistakes are natural
- balanced focus on message and form
- focus/feedback on message first
- writing for multiple audiences
- computer-mediated writing (email)

Choose one or two new items from the list above to implement across multiple writing tasks and activities.

2. Examine a broad range of school and local community issues with your students. Have students choose, research, and take appropriate social

Figure 6–3. Movement/pantomime activity. Grade 1 ELLs, beginning to early advanced, Martin School, South San Francisco, California. Teacher: author.

action on one issue (or several different issues if done in small groups). Stress the importance of pursuing interests of intense personal importance. Issues might range from the highly intractable, like prejudice, sexism, gang violence, and drugs, to still serious but more easily solved problems of graffiti, playground bullying, bad cafeteria food, inadequate school recycling, or the absence of a community animal shelter.

Depending on grade level and issue chosen, social actions might take a variety of forms: writing elected representatives, creating and performing an "awareness raising" puppet play for other classes, establishing an informational website, publishing a newsletter, launching a petition drive, or organizing a boycott.

Literacy building through social action is not for all teachers—and certainly not for the faint-hearted! If you go this route, expect potential flak from the administration and the occasional "What on earth are you doing!" call from parents. *Hint:* To eliminate (or greatly minimize) these problems, keep the principal and parents informed at each stage along the way.

3. Teachers like Victor who go a full-blown, write-for-real, process-based approach typically include student portfolios as an integral part of their writing program. Portfolios (collections of student work samples) are popular with teachers across most subject areas who decrease their use of skills-based materials. These teachers may keep some skills materials in the instructional mix, but no longer see them as the centerpiece or driving force of their program.

Teachers turn to portfolios for two reasons. One, for data to soothe the Powers That Be. If you're no longer using or relying exclusively on standardized tests and publishers' assessments, you need something concrete to show the principal, school board member, or state reviewer that students really *are* learning to write in their second language as they ruffle the feathers of city council members while militating for that traffic light or animal shelter. Portfolios fit the bill. Two, and most important, they work. Portfolios make students active participants in assessment and help teachers pinpoint strengths and weaknesses, plan appropriate activities and instruction, and monitor and document writing progress (Gottlieb 1995; Freeman and Freeman 1998).

If you've never used portfolios, take the plunge. Hints on implementation:

- Make sure students understand the *why*, *what*, and *how* of portfolio assessment.
- Make regular deposits of student work.
- Include a wide variety of work samples (brainstorming lists, graphic organizer outlines, skeletons, various drafts).
- Make sure deposits are made by teacher *and* students.
- Avoid the "skinny folder" syndrome where too little work is deposited to adequately document progress.
- Avoid the "black hole" syndrome where work goes in and is never reviewed or seen again.
- At a minimum, use a three-data-point review process (beginning, middle, end of unit/semester).
- Do periodic reviews—with the student!—to note growth, celebrate successes, and locate writing trouble spots.
- Make students an active part of the process, start to finish.

If you've been doing portfolio assessment for awhile, analyze your use, perhaps in terms of the hints above. Keep what's working and eliminate or modify what's not.

7

How do I teach grade-level content to English beginners?

READER'S GUIDE
English Language Learner Issue: Core curriculum access

Key Ideas
- Design programs around rich, engaging content
- Apply SDAIE strategies across all activities
- Use artifacts to boost content and language learning
- Emphasize collaborative over individual work
- Understand the differences between traditional, non-coordinated, and integrated ELD

Content:	Shoebox archaeology
Grade:	4
Teacher Experience:	1 year
ELL Language(s):	Spanish
School:	K–8, rural

The Classroom Story

ELDed to Death

Joellen took a deep breath. Before she left the principal's office, she was going to declare where she stood on ELD (English Language Development) instruction and see if Ms. Tessier stood with her or against her. It was a little early to rock the boat, but so be it. While student teaching in a different district, Joellen had seen kids run through ELD programs in both pull-out and in-class, pull-aside settings. The programs had been heavy on pronunciation practice and grammar-based worksheets and light on content. What subject matter there was never seemed to match the ongoing content of students' regular classrooms. As a first-year teacher,

Joellen was determined to help her English language learners avoid the social isolation and content loss she associated with traditional ELD instruction. But where was the principal with ELD? Would she support the sort of program Joellen envisioned, what her university field supervisor had called *integrated ELD?*

She and the principal were near the end of the get-acquainted talk Ms. Tessier had with each new hire at Grappelli Elementary. The talk had gone well thus far. Joellen had shared goals for the year and outlined her class management approach, then asked some questions related to materials and staff development. Ms. Tessier had discussed school culture and offered her help "whenever things get tough." The principal shifted in her chair and leaned forward. The talk was over. Now or never, thought Joellen. After another big breath and an excuse me for "one last item," she quickly summarized her experiences with English language learners during her student teaching assignments, mentioned her desire to go an integrated ELD route, and closed with the comment that she felt kids are sometimes "ELDed to death." How did the principal see it?

Big silence. Joellen waited, hoping she was still employed. The principal nodded slightly, which Joellen took as agreement with her "ELDed to death" statement, and said that like anything we do in the public schools, any program we run, there is always a potential downside, a possibility of turning a program in directions never intended and hurting kids when all we wanted to do was help them.

So far so good, no need to look for another job.

Joellen, Ms. Tessier explained, would have the chance to run the ELD component of her fourth-grade classroom as she saw fit—as long as she kept her eye on the bottom line: academically successful students. Half her class was English language learners, mostly students of Mexican heritage, with one youngster from El Salvador and another from Nicaragua. Six kids were at a beginning or early intermediate English level. Second language learners, like all students, the principal stressed, needed top-quality English skills to be successful. District-provided ELD materials were available; some teachers used them more than others.

The principal finished with a "Welcome aboard!" and another reminder to Joellen to attend to the English needs of her second language learners, but again told the new teacher that how she met those needs was her business as a professional. Joellen left the office thinking she and Ms. Tessier were on the same wavelength when it came to ELD, but time would tell.

Shoebox Archaeology

Initial assessments, literature activities, and an oceanography unit ate up most of the first five weeks of school. Going into week six, Joellen realized that she and the kids had done little in social studies. The state History–Social Science Content Standards (2006) told her fourth grade was California History and so she and the kids better get cracking. They would start with some shoebox archaeology and focus on the interaction between various Native American and settler groups. One of Joellen's master teachers had used historical artifacts to introduce his social studies units. Joellen was impressed by how much the artifacts stimulated an interest in history and by how much kids learned as they examined, researched, and finally identified the objects. Since then, she had begged, borrowed, and scrounged artifacts from friends and family for future use with her own students. She'd purchased a few other "gotta-have" items at flea markets, antique shows, and on eBay. A summer workshop at the county Office of Education gave her the shoebox idea, which looked like a great twist on the basic artifact investigation activity. In her lesson plans, Joellen labeled the two-week unit as *shoebox arch/ELD*. Part of the trick she knew would be dealing with that slash mark—making the unit workable and profitable for her English language learners. She had also invited Ms. Tessier to observe the unit activities any time she had a free moment.

On day one, Joellen divided the class into six archaeology teams and gave each team a plastic shoebox filled with compacted dirt. She kept explanations and directions to a minimum: Each box contained one artifact. The team task was to locate, excavate, and clean the object. All artifacts were real, rather than reproductions, and historically notable. Though no item was worth more than five or six dollars, some were fragile and could be damaged with rough handling. Archaeologists dig with care, she told the kids, so the number-one rule was BE CAREFUL!

Several students were already chomping at the bit and wanted to know what the objects were. Joellen told them sorry, but she was unable to say, since in the world of archaeology, archaeologists never know exactly what they will find until they start digging. She boiled all that down to "Dig and find out." The buried artifacts teams would soon excavate and later identify:

Team One: two "chevron" European glass beads from the 1600s
Team Two: three arrowheads, anywhere from one hundred and fifty to a
   thousand years old

Team Three: two spent bullets from the mid-nineteenth century
Team Four: a buffalo nickel with the date worn off (circa 1913–1938)
Team Five: a "penny" pipe from the mid-nineteenth century with a
broken stem
Team Six: an iron pothook from the mid-nineteenth century

Before setting the teams off on the dig, Joellen invited everyone to the center of the room for a fishbowl model. Four students joined her at a table for a "practice dig." The rest of the class stood in two concentric circles around the apprentice archaeologists. Circle people were to watch what the apprentice archaeologists did and how they did it. Joellen popped the lid on the shoebox, an extra she had packed for the modeling, and pulled several digging tools out of a plastic bag that lay on top of the dirt. She demonstrated how to use the tools—a fifteen-centimeter-long nail-probe for object location, a soup spoon and popsicle sticks for digging, and a small artist's brush for cleaning the artifact—then had the kids proceed with the dig, one person at a time, the student with the nail-probe going first.

Once the artifact—a small patent medicine bottle from the 1850s—was pinpointed in the shoebox, gingerly unearthed, and cleaned, Joellen asked her tablemates to examine it closely. As the object made the rounds, Joellen stopped students every now and then and asked them to think out loud and say what their senses were telling them. "What are you seeing . . . feeling . . . smelling . . . hearing . . . tasting?"

If the prompt sparked little or no description, Joellen took the bottle in her hand and generated a few descriptors herself. "Let's see. What am I seeing? . . . pale blue color, raised letters on one side, a little longer than my thumb; feeling? . . . smooth; smelling? . . . just dirt! . . . hearing? . . . a hollow sound when I tap; tasting?"

On the tasting prompt, Ernesto, who stood in the outside circle, made a "yuck face" and raised his hand. "Do we have to put these things in our mouth, Ms. Wilmot?"

Joellen tried to ease the boy's concern. "Well, no, probably not, but do whatever it takes to get the most information you can on your artifact. Use your senses—use your brain!"

Teams returned to their tables and began the dig. The teacher circulated, made sure kids followed excavation procedures, and helped with object description when needed. One student per group filled out an artifact description sheet, placing each descriptor in one of several categories, including size, shape, weight, color, and lettering/decoration. Joellen reminded several students that part of their job was to make sure everyone on the team understood the descriptors. Simply saying that an object had ridges, for example, would not be sufficient; the person needed to point to the features in question while verbally labeling them *ridges*.

Without any encouragement needed from the teacher, object description quickly turned to object hypothesizing. Angélica thought Team One's artifacts were tiny painted eggs with holes. Juan Pedro shook his head. "Son abalorios. [They're beads.]" Two members on Team Three were certain their artifacts were old fishing weights. Christopher said they could be "smashed pieces of a bike." Elvia nailed them: "Son balas." Martín quickly translated: "They're bullets." Team Four knew it had a U. S. coin worth five cents because of the writing on the back, but was not sure how old it was. Humberto said eight years old, Nora said fifty, and Jeremy two hundred. For sheer variety, Team Six's hypotheses were hard to beat. Initial guesses on their pothook ran from a cattle-branding tool and a sign letter to a roller coaster part and a Ninja "killing thing."

Joellen jumped on the hypothesizing. "OK, great, let's get these hypotheses—your best guesses—written down on something so we have a record of everybody's thinking."

Each group took a large sheet of paper, folded it in half three times to make eight boxes, and then wrote *Before Research* in big letters at the top. In the first six boxes students filled in answers to (1) What is it? (2) How old is it? (3) Where was it made? (4) What was it used for? (5) Who made it? and (6) Who used it? In the last two boxes, teams listed other questions they had about the artifact. For groups with competing "What is it?" hypotheses, which turned out to be all but the arrowhead and nickel groups, Joellen suggested they talk it out and try to come up with one best guess. If they couldn't, they were to take the top two guesses and fill out a *Before Research* sheet for each one. Again, the teacher reminded students of their responsibility to help "everybody contribute, everybody understand," regardless of how much English any team member had.

The next day, teams walked their objects around the room to give everyone a closer view and reported out best guesses. At this point, teams were instructed to carefully listen to one another, to begin thinking about how the objects might be connected, but to keep group-to-group questions and comments to a minimum. Questions and comments would come later, during the culminating activity—the Archaeology Convention.

In the morning, the class moved into a three-day research phase. Teams spent about an hour each day researching their objects and object-generated questions, and completing an *After Research* sheet containing the same questions answered during the best guess phase. Teams would use the before and after sheets to compare original hypotheses with their research-based findings. The sheets would also serve teacher and students as an assessment tool for partially measuring what and how much was learned during the unit. Students conducted research using six sources: (1) the school library; (2) the internet; (3) teacher-provided reference books and videos from the public library; (4) one nonteacher staff member at the school; (5) one community person (parents counting!); and (6) the class social studies text.

Ms. Tessier had observed during the digs and later agreed to be the non-teacher resource for Team Two. She had collected arrowheads as a girl scout and said she remembered a few facts that might help. The principal had also given Joellen two suggestions for other ways of documenting student progress during the archaeology unit: one, use her home video camera to sample small group work at beginning, mid, and ending points, and two, have each student keep an individual research log. Joellen liked and followed up on both suggestions. She had missed shots of the digs, and began the video portfolio with some of the before research sharing. The research log followed a simple *T* format, with the source and date on one side of the paper and notes on the other. Joellen modeled the note-taking format on the overhead, using facts about the medicine bottle excavated on the practice dig. The facts came from three sources: a website, a library book, and a friend of a friend who was a bottle collector.

Integrated ELD Sessions

Each day during the unit—but at nonunit times—Joellen pulled her six lowest-level English proficient students to a side table for a short ELD session. At each session, the teacher used and got the kids using some of the language needed for the day's unit activity. For example, one preview session dealt with descriptive vocabulary for the artifacts, another with a basic question structure kids could try out as they interviewed school personnel about their object. Other sessions used short video clips to provide background information on Native Americans and settler groups—information that other students were picking up through their reading and that was essential for identifying and connecting the shoebox artifacts. Another preview focused on "reading" the visuals in reference material and making *T* notes with pictures, key words, and short phrases. In three of the sessions, Joellen was able to incorporate some of the district-purchased ELD material.

The following week, groups shared the fruits of their research at the Grappelli Archaeology Convention. After reporting out answers to the basic "What is it?" and "How old is it?" questions, groups traded questions and comments. Joellen orchestrated the cross-talk and asked students to connect objects group to group. She also reminded teams several times to use the artifacts and any maps, graphs, or drawings they had prepared to "SHOW your point while you TELL your point," a phrase borrowed from Ms. Tessier who had used it while helping with one of the research sessions.

Team One had discovered that their European glass beads had made their way to Africa, then to America, and finally into the hands of the mountain men of the Far West in the 1840s. The team told how the mountain men used the beads for decoration and as trade goods with Native Americans. Later, they said, settlers might have used the bullets Team Three dug up to "shoot and just take what they wanted like furs and food." Wendy and Guillermina from Team Three acknowledged the "shoot and take" idea as a possibility, but favored the trade goods connection.

Team Five had learned how the Karoks of northern California had used tobacco for medical and ceremonial purposes. The team thought its penny pipe might have belonged to an early settler and been filled with "Indian tobacco." And if the settler had been wounded by one of Team Two's arrowheads or Team Three's bullets, they reasoned, the settler might have made a paste with some of the tobacco and used it as a pain killer. Gregorio from Team Two waved a hand and responded first with a couple phrases in English followed by several sentences in Spanish. Donald caught his team buddy's basic point and clarified for the teacher and the others: "The settlers needed to know how to use tobacco like the Karoks and maybe they never learned."

Sadness turned to outrage as the class listened to Team Four's description of the slaughter of the American buffalo. During the 1870s, special "excursion trains" carried tourists west and let them shoot all the animals they wanted through open coach windows. In 1800, there were about 60 million buffalo on the Great Plains. By 1913, when the group's nickel was first minted, the number had dropped to a few hundred. Sounding more like a prosecutor than an archaeologist, Alma declared that it was "possible" that Team Three's bullets killed one of those 60 million buffalo and that Team Six's iron pothook held a pot that cooked the meat.

"You can't say that!" shouted somebody from Team Three. Team Six joined in with a louder, "'Cause you don't know that for sure!" Another ten minutes of animated cross-talk followed on how the artifacts did (and did not!) connect to one another. Joellen chaired the convention one moment and refereed it the next when things got especially lively. Ms. Tessier listened, made notes, and shot some video at Joellen's request.

Postscript

About halfway through the unit, Joellen sat with the principal and reviewed how the year was going. Ms. Tessier commented on how much English and social studies content she thought Joellen's second language learners were picking up in the archaeology activities combined with the pull-aside, integrated ELD sessions.

Joellen, never one to hold back, popped the question: "So that kind of ELD is OK?"

"It is in my book," Ms. Tessier said, and laughed, "though some state school board members and a few state legislators might see it a little differently!"

Reflections

Three-Word Bomb

Toward the end of a recent workshop in the East Bay, one of the central office administrators popped in and joined the group and asked me to take a few moments to summarize my years of consulting work in the public schools. She wanted an overall impression of what I'd seen as a teacher coach hopping district to district around California and beyond. What had I learned about the public schools and English language learner instruction after observing in all those classrooms?

I told the group of K–12 teachers that I didn't need much time to synthesize my impressions; I could sum up my experiences in three words. The room grew quiet. Even the knitters, doodlers, and paper graders pushed aside their work and gave a listen. After the requisite dramatic pause, I dropped the bomb: "School is boring." I sat down. There was dead silence for a few seconds, then the room erupted in applause. Heads nodded their agreement.

I've been dropping the same little three-word bomb whenever I get the chance for several years now. Everybody always applauds. It's the applause of recognition, I think.

Teachers are bright folks; they know how unengaging school is. It's often tedious and painful, but only rarely is it exciting and relevant. They know much of what goes on in school is not real, not authentic. Teachers know deep down in their bones that marching kids year after year through skill-driven activities drained of high-interest content and emotion only makes sense if our goal is a skilled citizenry, not a skilled and thinking, creative citizenry. Teachers know that. They even applaud when someone like me in a blue blazer and a tie drops in from Consulting Land and reminds them that they know that. And yet, still, so much of school is boring. I remain an optimist, nevertheless, in large part because of teachers like Joellen and principals like Ms. Tessier—people committed to rich curriculum for all students, including English language learners, come hell or high water.

Joellen had seen a traditional, pull-out, grammar-based ELD program where English was listened to, repeated, sounded out, picked apart and put back together in a series of drills, games, worksheets, dictations, songs, chants, and dialogues—where kids practiced second language but rarely used it for real communication. The content of the program was language itself, with literature, math, science, history, and the arts in short supply. As an analogue, imagine an adult cooking class that taught pots, pans, utensils, and spices—but where nobody cooked.

Joellen had also observed a content-based ELD program. Content-based programs, in contrast to the traditional ELD variety, offer second language learners a chance to use and improve their English while acquiring subject matter concepts and skills (Brinton and Master 1997; Díaz-Rico and Weed 2006)—like learning how to use a whisk by making an omelet. But the subject matter of content-based programs, as Joellen found out, does not always match the content of the regular grade-level classroom. In these "noncoordinated" programs, students shuttle between two very different worlds of curriculum. Language and concepts gained in one setting are not automatically applied, strengthened, and stretched in the other. Staying with our cooking class analogy, we've gone to class, learned how to cook an omelet, then come home to a spouse and kids who won't touch eggs. We could whip up another omelet, but why bother?

Though most schools see the advantage of coordinated programs, noncoordinated programs abound, usually by default. Schools where few teachers have a background in second language theory and practice must typically funnel ELL kids to a specially trained resource teacher. The ELD pull-out teacher may work with several groups, each composed of students from different classrooms and sometimes different grades. Aligning ELD and grade-level activities across the various rooms and grades is a daunting and near impossible task, except on school-wide themes. Finally, Joellen was concerned about potential English learner segregation in both traditional and noncoordinated settings, with ELL and native English speakers dividing along *my program* versus *your program* lines.

Careful observation and reflection as a student teacher helped Joellen begin her teaching career clear on what she wanted for second language learners, regardless of their English proficiency—academic content, English skills, and full classroom inclusion. Her overriding question was never "Do I teach grade-level content or ELD?" but "How do I teach grade-level content *and* ELD?" Hence, the integrated ELD approach. To finish our analogy, integrated ELD was omelet cooking in a world of omelet cookers and eaters. Fortunately, Joellen had an ally in Ms. Tessier, who not only sanctioned the integrated ELD approach but helped her implement it as the year unfolded.

Implemention required making content engaging and workable for English language learners. No unit ever engages all kids, but Joellen's shoebox archaeology unit came close. Students were hooked by the digs, by the artifacts, and by the chance to work like historical detectives, like professional archaeologists. One reason student engagement was so high, Joellen felt, was because of the use of real artifacts rather than object reproductions or photos. I remembered watching one boy's eyes light up on learning that the beads he held in his hands were about four hundred years old, and knew she was right. Even the research phase held students' interest, though, granted, not quite to the degree the opening digs and hypothesizing had. Students researched alone and in pairs, used the various sources, kept notes, synthesized and discussed their findings in small groups, and did so throughout with care and enthusiasm. Joellen guided the research but never had to push it; kids pushed themselves along, driven by a genuine desire to find out what their artifact was and how it connected to the other artifacts in the room.

Yet Joellen's English language learners would never have kept pushing —and thus learning—had they found the unit activities incomprehensible. Making the activities understandable and doable for kids with low levels of English proficiency meant an extensive application of SDAIE (Specially Designed Academic Instruction in English) strategies and techniques, including:

- small, collaborative work groups
- bilingual peer bridges

- heavy use of objects, drawings, maps, and graphs
- "backgrounder" video clips
- reduced text note-taking
- authentic texts supported by multi-reading-level resource material
- show-and-tell modeling

The last item bears underscoring, since Joellen and I both felt her frequent and precise modeling played a big part in helping English learners succeed with the unit. Show-and-tell modeling gave kids a picture of what they were expected to do and how they were expected to do it. Imagine beginning-level ELD kids attempting artifact description after a tell-only model—or after several tell-only models. Tough going, to say the least.

In order to give teachers a feel for the drawbacks of tell-only modeling, I sometimes abruptly switch to Spanish in the middle of a workshop and describe what somebody in the group is wearing. I describe without showing what I'm describing, then ask questions about the description. The second time around, the person stands next to me while I point to and describe each item of clothing—blue sweater, gold necklace, beige slacks, and short-heeled shoes, for example. Folks with little or no Spanish find the exercise slightly jarring, but tolerable and even amusing if I quickly follow the tell-only description with the show-and-tell model. When I save the show-and-tell model for later, however, and run through several back-to-back tell-only descriptions, things turn ugly. Participants squirm, stop listening, and send mild curses my direction. Twice, I've had people leave the room.

Finally, after the show-and-tell model, we talk about what was just experienced. For many, the "What's he saying?!" activity is an eye opener. Teachers comment on the inherent language-building power of hooking words to objects and actions (Asher 1977; Seely and Romijn 1995; Cary 1998), but many also say how frustrated and angry they felt during the tell-only descriptions. Teacher talk quickly shifts to describing how much frustration and anger English beginners must feel when the "show" component is missing—not for four or five minutes as it was during the workshop, but for hours at a stretch in school.

Joellen also made the shoebox archaeology activities more understandable through several pull-aside ELD sessions. Consistent with an integrated (aka, coordinated) content-based approach, the WHAT of each session matched the WHAT of a shoebox archaeology activity. In other words, fourth-grade core curriculum, rather than an English as a Second

Language scope and sequence, determined what students did in ELD. Though content-driven, each session had one or more clearly defined English language skill objectives, for example, using size, color, and texture vocabulary, posing yes-no versus open-ended questions, note-taking via drawings and short labeling, or writing sentences with a comparison structure.

Teachers new to integrated ELD often worry about choosing the "right" language objective for a session. I always suggest they look at an upcoming content activity and ask themselves one key question: "What will kids need to DO with language in the activity?" The answer to that question automatically carries teachers to specific English listening, speaking, reading, and writing skills that can be modeled by the teacher and content-applied by the students in one or more ELD sessions. Knowing what particular skills are needed for activity success also helps teachers decide on which parts of a commercially published set of ELD materials to incorporate and which parts to set aside for future use.

As Joellen and the principal reflected on their activity observations and reviewed research logs and the video portfolio, it was clear that second language learners had learned a lot of social studies content and English during the unit. Not all social studies concepts were 100 percent understandable, of course, for beginning English kids. Reaching that level would have required large amounts of primary language instruction. Nothing beats a student's first language for concept development, which is one reason—of many—I'm such a big fan of bilingual education. Research has clearly shown that students in bilingual programs do as well as and typically outperform their all-English program peers in English and academic achievement (Krashen 1996; Rolstad, Mahoney, and Glass 2005; Slavin and Cheung 2005). And students in bilingual programs end their K–12 journey with a major life and job market advantage: proficiency in *two languages*, a fact that's often downplayed or disregarded altogether by the English-only side in the debate over bilingual education. Unfortunately, most schools and districts around the country offer little to no primary language instruction for their ELL students, either because they can't find the credentialed bilingual teachers they need or because they can't find the political courage and consensus to make bilingual education a reality.

Without formal bilingual education, however, Joellen was still able to make many of the social studies concepts understandable—Westward expansion, the environment determining living patterns, trade dynamics, bicultural conflict, assimiliation versus acculturation, for example—many more than would have been the case without the application of SDAIE strategies and techniques, including bilingual peer help.

Joellen, with the principal's ongoing support, had stayed true to her original integrated ELD vision: English language learners had been where the "action" was—in the core curriculum of the grade-level classroom—socially and academically throughout the unit. ELD instruction had helped with inclusion, not hindered it.

Postscript

I visited with Joellen before school one morning a few weeks after the shoebox archaeology unit had ended. We played the One Thing game—trying to name that one item that was most responsible for the unit's success—the one thing that the unit could not have lived without. We both knew the success of the unit depended on a variety of factors, but playing the game we quickly agreed that it was the artifacts. Take away everything else, but leave us the goodies, the rich content.

A final plug for high-interest curriculum: I keep a Peanuts cartoon strip taped to the top of my Macintosh and often refer to it when trying to decide what to share with teachers in a workshop or with students in a demo activity. In the strip, Rerun sits at a school desk and starts to read the class an exciting story he's written about "this kid who's in Kindergarten and how the stress is slowly destroying him." The teacher stops him mid-sentence, finding the story a little too controversial and a little too close to home, and suggests he switch topics. Rerun hangs his head, dispirited, and says, "Well, I have another one here about some purple bunnies."

Joellen won't do purple bunnies, and I'm happy and proud to report, neither will I.

Discussion and Application

Discussion

1. Using the definitions from the chapter, mark where your school- or district-wide ELD program falls on the ELD Program Continuum (Figure 7–1). Cite evidence to justify where you've located the program. An interesting, eye-opening option: Place two marks on the continuum, one based on your firsthand knowledge of the program, the other on the school or district's formal description of it. Again, cite evidence for each mark. Do the two marks fall at the same point, meaning the program you have is the program the school and district say you have? Or are the

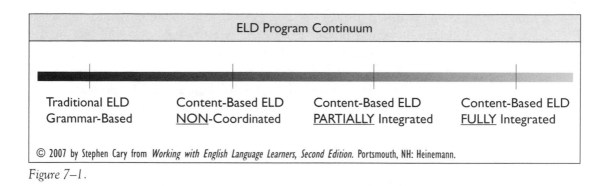

Figure 7–1.

marks far apart? If far apart, what do you and colleagues need in terms of materials, staff development, and human resources to make program reality match program promise?

2. Think about how you help your beginning and early intermediate English learners access grade-level content. What strategies are you using? How would you characterize their effectiveness? Are they giving full access? partial? minimal access? Keep in mind the difference between *offering* access and *giving* it. Offering is passive, for example, using heterogeneous groups and assuming native speakers will help nonnative speakers. Giving access is active. With those same heterogeneous groups, we take time to explain the rationale of peer assistance and model what that looks and sounds like within a small group structure. Once an activity is underway, we move group to group and check to make sure students who need help with language and content learning are getting it. If not, we intervene and provide the help—and another model of helping—ourselves.

A second example: Offering access means we encourage English beginners to find and read some background material on the Web in their primary language related to an upcoming social studies topic. Giving access means we encourage L1 reading, assist in locating appropriate websites, and—if we don't speak the students' primary language—arrange for a peer buddy, instructional aide, or community volunteer to serve as a bilingual student-to-teacher bridge so students can demonstrate knowledge and pose questions about the reading. In short: offering access is relatively easy; giving access takes some doing.

3. Reflect on the amount and type of modeling you usually do for a new curriculum unit. Do you model each activity in the unit or only one or

two potentially "troublesome" activities? Are you doing all one-shot models or sometimes repeating models? Are most models tell-only or the show-and-tell variety favored by Joellen? Are most models directed to the whole class or to small groups? How would you rate the effectiveness of your modeling in terms of helping English language beginners learn grade-level content? If your modeling is less than stellar, what elements need changing to increase effectiveness?

Application

1. Consider the rich mix of instructional approaches, strategies, and techniques Joellen used within the shoebox achaeology unit:

- inquiry-based history
- manipulative-based (artifact-driven) history (Figures 7–2 and 7–3)
- multimodal teaching/exploration (Figure 7–4)
- small group collaboration
- pair work, peer assistance
- encouraging L1 as a learning tool
- fishbowl modeling
- show-and-tell modeling

Figure 7–2. Artifacts for shoebox archaeology, clockwise: chevron beads, arrowheads, buffalo nickel, clay pipe, spent bullets.

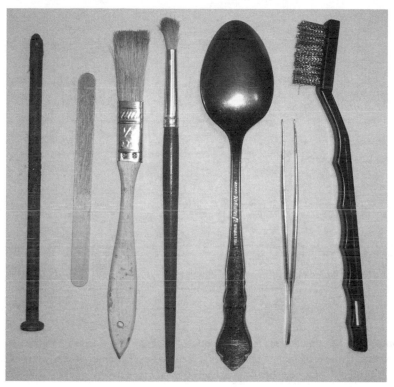

Figure 7–3. Tools for shoebox archaeology, left to right: nail probe, Popsicle® stick, artist brushes, spoon, tweezers, wire brush.

- key vocabulary targets
- multisource researching
- reduced-text note taking (with drawings) (Figure 7–5)
- multimodal authentic assessment (observation, group research sheets, individual research logs, video portfolios)

No single item above is golden. Show-and-tell modeling or peer assistance alone, for example, will help with access but won't guarantee it. Most teachers find they need multiple strategies to bring grade-level content to English beginners. Take a multiple-strategy route with your next unit. Borrow a couple items from Joellen's bag of instructional tricks and add them to your own. Monitor the level of content learning with the new strategies. If you're still not getting the content bang you're after, add one or two additional strategies or rework existing ones, for example, by increasing the amount of L1 support material, hooking more pictures

Figure 7–4. Multimodal artifact description. Text based on small group discussion and shared writing. Grade 3 ELL, early intermediate, Clarendon Elementary School, San Francisco, California. Student teacher: Caryn Hoadley.

to key vocabulary, or training students on how (and how not!) to help a peer buddy.

2. Artifacts don't have to be old and historically significant like Joellen's. Remembering that an artifact is simply any object made by humans, we've got plenty to choose from. Artifacts—all artifacts—are inherently appealing. Unlike abstract text, artifacts provide a concrete experience. And hands-on, concrete experiences engage more of our senses, building stronger neural connections through mulitple pathways in the brain. The upshot: students have more ways to store and recall information (Wolfe 2001).

Some artifacts, like the Bazooka® Bubble Gum I recently used with a group of third-grade English learners to teach descriptive vocabulary (and ultimately story character description), engage *every* sense. The teacher-sanctioned gum chewing activated the sense of sight (pink and white), hearing (pop!), touch (sticky), smell (sweet), and taste (yummy!). And as a fun, literacy-building bonus, we got to read the

(BEFORE RESEARCH)

| what? → bullet ??? | How old? ⟵ 2004 |
| | 300 years |

| where made? | Used for? BOOM! |
| D.F.—Mexico City | Fight revolution— Kill bad people |

| who made it? | who used it? |
| company — gun | soldier — Army — Air Force ??? — Villa — Zapata |

Questions	⑥ Black ring inside?
① What's knob do? ④ Rings?	⑦ Kind of metal?
② Smell inside? ⑤ what gun?	⑧ Why did top break?
③ Picture of women?	⑨ Bigger size? — now
	⑩ Cost? ⑪ Dangerous?

Figure 7–5. Graphic organizer with support drawings. Type: note-taking grid. Teacher-created at overhead based on student input after initial artifact investigation. Artifact: early 20th-century lipstick holder (not a 300-year-old bullet!). Grade 6 ELLs, early intermediate to advanced, Franklin School, San Jose, California. Teacher: author.

Figure 7–6.

111

Figure 7–7. Bazooka Joe comic. Gum as a multimodal language and literacy builder!

Bazooka Joe comics wrapped around each piece of gum (Figure 7–7). A second example: I remember traveling in Mexico many years ago as a Spanish beginner and discovering small, whimsical skeleton figures in one of the open-air markets. Some were dressed as musicians, some as brides and grooms, others as truck drivers or ranchers, all pursuing life, but all with skull heads. I was fascinated. I had to know the name of this wonderful folk-craft (*muertos*), and quickly gathered enough vocabulary and relevant structures to ask about their history, production, and contemporary use in Mexico's Día de los Muertos celebration.

Those experiences coupled with Joellen's shoebox archaeology unit remind us that artifacts spur second language use and development. Equally important, artifacts help make school interesting and relevant, no small feat in an era where engaging content is often squeezed out by a school or district's obsession with pacing schedules, scripted learning, high-stakes testing, and, in Alfie Kohn's marvelously apt phrase, standards on steroids (Kohn 2001).

Take an upcoming activity and contextualize it with a number of artifacts. If possible, choose an activity you've done before but have never done with objects as key components. Note the impact the artifacts have on English beginners' level of engagement, content learning, and quantity and quality of second language use.

Integrated ELD Review Chart			
Element	**Current Status** (circle)		
Number of sessions	too few	too many	just right
Structure	too loose	too rigid	just right
Pacing	too slow	too fast	just right
Focus on content	too little	too much	just right
Focus on language	too little	too much	just right
Commercial ELD material	too little	too much	just right
Staff collaboration	too little	too much	just right
Learning documentation	too little	too much	just right
Content/L2 learning	minimal	moderate	substantial

© 2007 by Stephen Cary from *Working with English Language Learners, Second Edition.* Portsmouth, NH: Heinemann.

Figure 7–8.

3. If you're at a school with an integrated ELD program, review your own pull-aside sessions per the Integrated ELD Review Chart (Figure 7–8). Modify any elements you find wanting to increase the effectiveness of the sessions.

If you're at a school without an integrated ELD program and you believe such a program would help students learn more language and grade-level content:

1. Combine forces with a couple colleagues who support the idea.
2. Research and visit local schools with established integrated programs.
3. Put together a miniproposal briefly spelling out the rationale, program design, and key action steps needed to make the program a reality.
4. Share the proposal with principal, faculty, and parent groups for consideration and feedback.

8

How do I help students build learning strategies?

READER'S GUIDE
English Language Learner Issue: Learning to learn; academic competence

Key Ideas
- Integrate and teach learning strategies across the curriculum
- Emphasize reading comprehension strategies
- Make learning strategies immediately applicable
- Use a variety of SDAIE strategies and techniques
- Understand the differences between strategy-to-content and content-to-strategy approaches

Content:	Airplane design, building, testing
Grade:	5
Teacher Experience:	28 years
ELL Language(s):	Spanish, Cantonese, Punjabi, Farsi
School:	K–5, suburban

The Classroom Story

Clutter Champion

Dougie Mullins called it the "Dump." After seventeen years as a district custodian, the last four at Blakey Elementary, Dougie had seen his share of messy classrooms. But Mrs. Chen's took the prize, hands down. Nice lady, Dougie thought, but imagining what the inside of her house must look like gave him the creeps. Dougie sometimes admitted he was clean and tidy to a fault, but you could eat off the floors at his house any day of the week.

It was close to 6:30 P.M. and Blakey was deserted. In the East Wing hallway Dougie paused by Mrs. Chen's door, took a deep breath, steeled himself, and pushed a wide broom across the threshold and into the Dump.

Navigating the room was always difficult. Mrs. Chen had outgrown the storage cabinets long ago; books, folders, old student projects, games, broken AV equipment, science gear, and art material were deposited around the periphery of the room in tall piles that often gave way and sent their contents tumbling across the floor. Spills from cooking and science experiments gone bad were common. But the room was extra trashy today. The floor was littered with papers, some crumpled into little balls, most folded once or twice and then discarded.

Mrs. Chen had gotten the kids to clean up a lot of the papers—the three trash cans were overflowing—but had left a couple dozen spillover items near the cans for Mr. Mullins. Completed paper airplanes of various sizes and shapes lined the back counter. Dougie rolled his eyes. Here we go again, he thought. This was Monday. He knew he'd be sweeping up crumples for a week until the "plane thing" was over.

The next day, Fiona Chen's fifth graders quickly moved into their aerospace design teams. Mrs. Chen dashed from group to group, checking on last-minute flight test preparations; kids had to be in and out of the gym by 2:15. Fiona still wore tennies from her lunch walk. She was nearly sixty with short-cropped gray hair and could outwalk—and outwork—most Blakey teachers half her age. Her energy and zest, she kidded colleagues, came from flying. She was a small-plane pilot, and getting closer to the sun each weekend provided a power boost. Fiona had been sharing her love of flying via the plane design unit for years. The unit provided several good spots to work on learning strategies, an integral part of everything she did in the classroom.

Fiona was working with eight nonnative English speakers this year from four language groups: Spanish, Cantonese, Punjabi, and Farsi. All had "FEPed out," district parlance for second language learners who had reached Fluent English Proficient status based on several criteria, including a fluent score on a state-approved English language proficiency test. Though the students' English oral skills were very good to excellent, literacy skills were far from native level. Gaining some solid reading comprehension strategies would be critical for these eight if they were to ever "step up" to grade-level reading and become top-notch, independent learners.

Strategy Talk

During days one and two of the unit, students folded and tested plane models called "The Dart," "The Square," and "The Hornet" from *The*

World Record Paper Airplane Book by Ken Blackburn and Jeff Lammers (1994). Each model was built from a single sheet of 8½- by-11-inch paper, and without scissors, paper clips, or tape. At the start, Fiona told the class that good model builders needed to follow directions, and to do that, you had to understand the directions you were trying to follow. She placed the plans for the Dart on the overhead and asked, "What sort of reading strategy could we use to make sense of these directions?" The page contained nine separate steps. Each step was numbered and had a picture beside it illustrating the fold. The students offered a variety of strategies.

"Read each direction twice so you don't miss something important," Lydia suggested.

"Look at the pictures," said Georgina.

Patrick expanded on Georgina's strategy: "Yeah, but look at the last picture first."

"Why the last picture first?" the teacher asked.

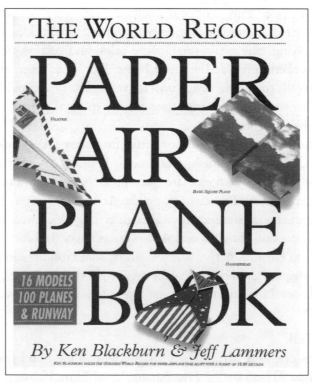

Figure 8–1.

Figure 8–2. Paper airplanes, left to right: Dart, The Square, Hornet, Raptor, Interceptor. Based on designs from The World Record Paper Airplane Book *(Blackburn and Lammers 1994). Grade 4–6 ELLs, beginning to advanced levels, various San Francisco Bay Area schools, California.*

Patrick thought a second. "'Cause it shows you what you get at the end. How the plane is supposed to look."

Fiona then told how she sometimes "jump reads": reads the last couple paragraphs of a newspaper or magazine article to see "how the story comes out."

Another hand went up. "Look at the pictures *and* read the directions," offered Derrick, stressing the *and*.

"Why do both?" the teacher wondered.

Chee jumped in: "The picture tell something we need to know and the word some other thing, and you have the picture and word and you make this fold better."

Agustín had one more strategy: "Ask Juan Diego how to do it—he makes good planes!" Juan Diego perked up in the back of the room and grinned.

Fiona laughed and admitted that was a good strategy all right, but Juan Diego would be too busy in his own group to show everybody how to make the Dart.

She drew the strategy talk to a close. "OK, so we've got several ways to read this thing. Which strategy makes the most sense for this particular kind of reading?"

Kids decided going the pictures-plus-words route would be best. They also agreed that looking at the last picture first was a good way to start out.

Reading Strategies

On day three, teams read a seven-page research handout on plane design and aerodynamics that included sections on weight, lift, drag, thrust, and stability. The handouts had a few visuals but were far more text-heavy than the model directions. Before the reading began, Fiona underscored the purpose of the reading: to get more design and flight know-how information. Teams would put what they learned from the handout with what they had learned from the first two days of model building and testing to design an original entry for Friday's Super Fly-Off. Ribbons and a write-up in the school paper would go to team winners in three categories: Longest Flight, Longest Time Aloft, and Most Accurate Flight.

The teacher walked to one of the side whiteboards and grabbed a marker. "One thing researchers do to make more sense of what they're reading is to organize the material as they read it—they keep notes. Any ideas," Fiona asked the class, "on how we can take notes on the plane handout?"

Students shared several possibilities, each one a different type of graphic organizer that Fiona had modeled previously and that kids had applied in other activities. After a little discussion, students felt two types would work best for the kind of information they were after: a fish bone map and a basic box chart. Both would allow students space for definitions of key flight/design terms and also provide a good visual display of cause and effect relationships, for example: elevator up or down equals pitch stability; rudder left or right equals directional stability. Groups read the handout in pairs with each pair deciding which organizer to use. The teacher circulated during the reading, moving pair to pair, helping with the note-taking and modeling other reading comprehension strategies when needed.

Fiona sat down next to Qianying and Milly. Milly, a native English speaker, read out loud, stopped, scribbled notes inside a box chart, then came back to the reading and charged ahead. Qianying listened through it all but said little. At the next note-taking stop, the teacher asked, "How can you make sure both of you are understanding what you're reading?"

"Take turns reading," answered Milly.

"Well, you could take turns, sure. But I can read something and still not understand it."

"I ask Milly questions," Qianying said.

"Yes, that's a good strategy—asking questions about the reading. I can ask myself if I understand the section or I can ask my reading partner if she understands. Together we can figure the reading out. Maybe we have to reread a part or find out what a word means, like here, where it says *elevators*. Are you OK on *elevators?*"

Qianying shook her head.

"So that's a word you need to ask about, talk about, because it's used about a hundred times in here!"

Fiona suggested they also alternate the note-taking and then moved on to another pair. A quick glance at Jill and Rajiv's notes showed they were not understanding the handout section on stability. Fiona suggested a rereading using a strategy of *visualization:* "This time, stop a couple times in the section and try to make a picture in your head about what you're reading."

The pair reread the section and tried to make pictures.

"Are the pictures clear or fuzzy?" Fiona asked.

"Fuzzy," both confessed. The kids were having difficulty sorting out the three types of stability: pitch, directional, and spiral.

"OK, what strategy do you use now?" Fiona asked.

Jill answered first: "Maybe *resourcing*—look at one of the plane books in the room and see if there's pictures or something good on pitch and like that."

"Or ask somebody for help," Rajiv added, "and see if they understand the part."

"Yeah, good strategies," Fiona said. "Or . . . maybe *using prior knowledge*. Think about flying those first test models. You've already seen the types of stability—and instability—in action. Think about what you already know about that section."

After the handout reading, pairs returned to their teams and shared and compared information.

On day four, groups designed and built their Fly-Off planes. Before heading to the gym for flight tests, Fiona asked the class, "What procedures do we need to follow to get good data so we can make modifications, make our planes fly better? What strategies would good aerospace engineers use?" Students agreed on a set of procedures, which Fiona wrote inside a box flowchart on the board. For data gathering and crunching, they chose the *double-check* strategy. Two students would independently gather and calculate all flight test results, including lift/drag ratios.

Day five: It was 10:15 and the Super Fly-Off wasn't till 11:00, but kids were already putting away their current event work and asking if they could get into their design teams. Fiona went with the prevailing wind; kids could always return to the current event geography questions on Monday.

Students made last-minute adjustments to their planes: Fuselage, nose, rudder, wings, wing tips, and elevator tabs were tweaked, smoothed out, creased, recreased, and tweaked again. Then all the groups checked their flight test logs one last time. Logs showed data on models tested over the past four days and had to include all distance, duration, and accuracy measurements, totaled and averaged across each plane's trials. Data recorded during the Fly-Off would complete the logs. No team could win a prize at the flight competition without "proper documentation"—complete and accurate flight test log data.

At the Super Fly-Off, Team Two's Rocket Hawk won for Longest Flight. Team Five's Screamin' Jay flew three and a half seconds longer than Team One's Baddy Bird to take the Time Aloft award. Zoom Machine's precision flying earned Team Four the ribbon for Most Accurate Flight.

The principal and three parents served as "flight managers" and helped the teacher present each student in the competition with an "International Paper Airplane Pilot License" and an official I Flew in the Blakey Fly-Off certificate.

Postscript

Early Monday evening, Dougie Mullins was back in the Dump. He looked around the room. No overflowing trashcans. No paper crumples on the floor. Good, he thought; that's it for the "plane thing." At the back of the room, his left shoe suddenly sank into something squishy—and stinky. He winced, then looked down. He wasn't sure if it was a pear or a mango, it was so far gone. Dougie scraped the goo off and reminded himself to tread lightly till Mrs. Chen's "rotting fruit science thing" petered out.

Reflections

Starting with Content

At some point, when the topic turns to what we want for kids, not just this year but at the very end of the school line, nearly every teacher I've ever worked with has mentioned kids becoming independent learners: And independent learners require tons of learning strategies.

Consistent with theory and research on learning strategy instruction (Chamot and O'Malley 1994, 1996; Carrier 2003; Chamot 2005), Fiona made those strategies explicit, teaching them rather than assuming students would pick them up one by one as they marched through the system. She wanted to equip all students with learning strategies, of course, but was especially concerned, she told me, about strategies for her English language learners. She worried about the plateau kids, students who reached an intermediate fluency stage and stayed there, spinning their learning wheels, never rising to native-level English proficiency, never achieving full academic competence.

Boosting the kids up a notch to academic competence is a tall order for any teacher, even one as experienced and energized as Fiona. Besides English proficiency, academic competence demands lavish amounts of declarative knowledge—the WHAT of learning—all the cultural and subject matter facts. It also demands a hefty load of procedural knowledge—the HOW of learning—all the operations and processes, all the higher-order thinking and learning skills that most of us simply call learning strategies.

Fiona targeted reading comprehension strategies as often as she could, knowing that many of her English language learners still struggled to make sense of text. She also knew reading was the number one skill students would need to succeed in middle school, high school, college, and beyond. A teacher not working on reading would be a lot like a musician not working on rhythm; it was central, and Fiona had been working on reading strategies for years.

Yet how she taught reading comprehension and other learning strategies changed considerably during our coaching work together. At the start, Fiona followed a strategy-to-content approach, working from a master list of metacognitive, cognitive, and social-affective strategies picked up at a conference a decade ago. She took a strategy from the list each week, did a few minutes of direct instruction modeling, then had kids apply the strategy in an activity. The content of the activity was beside the point. What was important was applying and learning the strategy.

Fiona felt the approach did some good, but was concerned with the lack of student "buy-in"; kids frequently groaned when she announced it was strategy time. And she was not seeing the strategies being used as much as she wanted in activities outside the formal teaching sessions. She wanted to go a different direction, but still do some direct, large group instruction on strategies along the way.

As our coaching relationship evolved, Fiona moved to a content-to-strategy approach. With this approach, Fiona started with content—high-interest, grade-level content. After deciding on the paper airplane unit, she asked herself what kids needed to know (declarative knowledge) and what they needed to do (procedural knowledge) to be successful with the activities. The answers to those questions—understand the model directions, take notes on the research handout, record and organize flight test data—pointed directly to specific learning strategies she needed to highlight, either through whole class direct instruction or through small group or pair modeling.

With the content-driven approach, kids learned to use a fish bone map, for example, not because such a map might come in handy some day, but as a tool for learning something they needed and wanted to learn about RIGHT NOW. Making the strategy relevant got Fiona the student "buy-in"—the emotional investment in the strategy—she was after. She knew that emotion drives attention and attention drives learning; the more emotionally connected students felt to the material, the more concepts and skills learned (Sylwester 1995; Wolfe 2001). Needing the fish bone map increased attention to the map, and attention to the map helped kids learn it. Then, immediately applying the map to high-interest content reinforced the strategy and increased the likelihood that the fish bone would be added to a student's long-term strategy stash for later use.

Fiona never assumed, however, that the immediate and enthusiastic application of a strategy in one setting would guarantee its application in another. She "talked strategies" across the curriculum, reminding kids, for example, that the visualization and self-questioning strategies they found helpful in reading the handout on aerodynamics would be just as helpful in their book groups when reading *Sing Down the Moon* (O' Dell 1997) or *My Brother Sam Is Dead* (Collier and Collier 2005). And the same strategies could—and probably should—be applied in doing those math word problems on perimeter and finding the area of a triangle. And why not try them out on that Shel Silverstein poem so you know what he's really saying!

Giving learning strategies names—resourcing, using prior knowledge, the double-check, the jump-read—helped make them explicit and memorable. Fiona also had the strategy names posted above the front whiteboard, each numbered and written in big blue letters. She would occasionally be working with a pair or group, glance up at the strategy chart, and tell kids it looked like a number three or a number eight might be needed here or there.

Of course, like anything we do in the classroom, we can beat kids to death with learning strategies. In our coaching sessions, Fiona and I wrestled with the "How much is too much?" question. Fiona went back to what was driving the chosen approach—content—and decided on a simple guideline: She would back off strategy instruction, strategy talk, and strategy reminders when it got in the way of content.

Vicente provides a good example. On day four of the plane unit, teams were at the airfield gym testing their Fly-Off models. As Vicente was preparing his group's plane for the first test flight, Fiona asked him what strategy the team was going to use to make sense of the data. Vicente shrugged his shoulders; he didn't know.

"How about categorizing?" Fiona asked. "Or compare and contrast?"

No response. Fiona ticked off a few more possibilities: "Pair talk? Summarizing? Maybe verification?"

Again, Vicente shrugged, and then told her the team didn't have any data. They had to "fly the plane first," he said.

Fiona and I decided that if Vicente ever runs for school board, he has our vote.

Whole Lotta Buzzin' Goin' On

Fiona's room buzzed with learning. Kids were actively involved in the WHAT and the HOW, constructing knowledge and all the processes they would need—the learning strategies—to get that knowledge. Unfortunately, not all rooms buzz. In fact, some don't even softly murmur. When working with a teacher from a buzzless or mostly buzzless room, I try to shift one of our early conversations away from the classroom and into the teacher's life. I ask what he or she does for kicks outside school—the hobby, the burning passion—and then gently suggest that passion as a starting point for moving to higher-interest, buzz-inducing curriculum.

Fiona's airplane unit buzzed because Fiona loved airplanes. Her ripening fruit unit buzzed because she loved anything and everything connected to science experimentation. She taught what she loved, obviously not five or six hours a day throughout the year, but whenever she could educationally justify it. She also made sure student hobbies and interests were incorporated into the program whenever possible. In short, the room buzzed with learning because teacher and students pursued lots of topics they were genuinely interested in.

With relevant topics in place, Fiona could decide on how best to make the topics workable for English learners—on strategies for learning content and learning language through content. But, again, the beginning point was content, not skills, not strategies.

Postscript

Here's a little sympathy for Mr. Mullins. Buzzing, active, hands-on classrooms like Fiona's are notoriously messy. Some are worse than others, and I'm afraid Mr. Mullins was right; Fiona's classroom was a dump. Granted, one of the best spots to learn I've ever come across, but a dump. Nobody's perfect.

Discussion and Application

Discussion

1. Reflect on how you're helping your second language students develop strategies for independent learning. Like Fiona, do you explicitly teach learning strategies with most instructional units, or favor an implicit, strategies-by-osmosis approach? How would you rate the effectiveness of your current approach? Are students building an ever increasing stock of strategies? Do you see them successfully applying new strategies in a variety of academic settings?

2. If you teach learning strategies, consider what drives strategy selection. I recently watched a middle school SDAIE biology teacher lecture his class of English learners on one of the most important learning strategies in science—classifying, making sense of the world through the systematic division of phenomena based on observed similarities and differences. He spent a full period talking kingdom, phylum, class, order, family, genus, and species. There were plenty of visuals and clear explanations, but no student application of the strategy. Students

listened politely, responded to questions, but for the most part, were about as engaged as soccer fans at a croquet tournament. Students wouldn't have a chance (or a real need) to classify anything until lab time, which was over a week away. But the commercial science text the teacher was using said teach biological taxonomy that day and so he dutifully taught biological taxonomy.

Another teacher in the same science department told me she had "reworked" the curriculum and immediately followed a short classification talk and note-taking model with the lab the same day, explaining that students needed to know the basics of classifying and how to take notes "to do OK with the lab." The first teacher worked strategy-to-content, the second content-to-strategy.

If you've been using a strategy-to-content approach and would like to do more content-to-strategy teaching, what do you need to consider in terms of curriculum, instruction, and assessment to make the switch? What problems are you likely to face as you implement the new approach? What are possible solutions to those problems?

3. Learning strategies are frequently pigeon-holed into three major categories: metacognitive, cognitive, and social-affective (Chamot and O'Malley 1994). Metacognitive strategies are global in nature and help us plan, monitor, and assess our learning. Examples: Sequencing the steps in a science experiment, regularly posing the "Am I understanding this?" question while reading academic text, and keeping a math learning log to document skill building. Cognitive strategies are more specific in nature and help us successfully complete particular tasks. Examples: Doing a Google search for kid-friendly articles on endangered species protection using keywords and quotes, summarizing and retelling an oral story or read-aloud chapter via storyboarding (Figure 8–3), increasing comprehension of primary source history material using context clues, prediction, and visualization. Social-affective strategies help students collaborate and learn with others. Examples: Asking a classmate for an explanation of an idiom, sharing an opinion about a political issue in a small group, and—especially critical for English language learners—giving yourself reminders to risk making errors in L2, to focus on message over form.

Consider the types of strategies you're highlighting during a typical week's activities. Are you hitting strategies from all three categories? If not, what area or areas need more attention?

125

Figure 8–3 Storyboard, after listening to teacher-told oral story, "Stay Away from Trouble." Grade 3 ELL, intermediate, Franklin School, San Jose, California.

Application

1. Fiona focused on a number of important reading comprehension strategies within the airplane design unit, including:

- self-questioning
- rereading
- picture-plus-word reading
- jump-reading (last part first)
- visualization
- buddy reading
- note-taking with graphic organizers (Figures 8–4 and 8–5)
- note-taking with flow charts
- tapping prior knowledge

For an upcoming unit, consider what students will need to read. Based on the nature and difficulty of the reading, choose a couple strategies from the list above that could increase comprehension of the material. Then explicitly teach those strategies within the unit using Fiona's approach as a guide, remembering to:

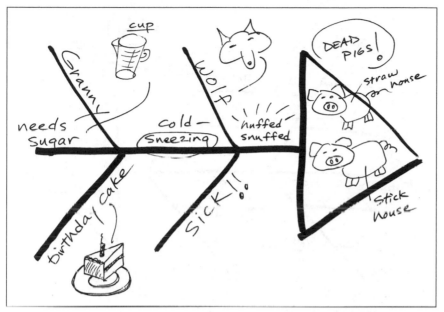

Figure 8–4. Graphic organizer with support drawings. Type: fishbone (cause and effect). Teacher-created at overhead after picture walk, read-aloud, and discussion, The True Story of the 3 Little Pigs! *(Scieszka and Smith 1989). Grade 1–2 ELLs, beginning to intermediate, Franklin School, San Jose, California. Teacher: author.*

- name the strategy
- model (and remodel)
- give real-world examples of application
- provide pair, small group, and independent application
- compare and contrast strategies (What's best for X task?)
- look for ways of using strategies across the curriculum

2. Teachers often feel overwhelmed by the sheer number of concepts and skills they're expected to teach in a year. Given curriculum demands, some teachers omit explicit work on learning strategies altogether. Others squeeze the work in, but rush through it. Teachers in "rush mode" may leave out a crucial step in strategy teaching: student self-assessment, giving students the time and means to determine (1) what strategies they're using to help themselves learn, (2) to what degree the strategies are helping, and if not helping, (3) what other strategies they might try.

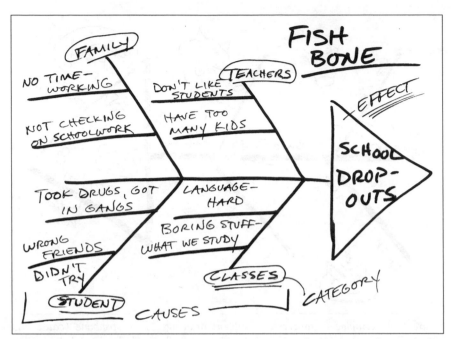

Figure 8–5. Graphic organizer. Type: fishbone (cause and effect). Teacher-created at overhead after short readings and small group discussions on school dropouts. Grade 11 ELLs, intermediate to advanced, San Francisco Bay Area high school, California. Teacher: author.

At the end of an upcoming activity—and when you're out of "rush mode"—have students assess their use of a particular strategy. See Figure 8–6 for the learning strategy assessment form I use with upper-grade elementary students. Use this form or one modified for your particular grade level and target strategies. Students can fill out the form either individually or with a peer buddy. There's no need to assess after every activity. Consider using the forms once or twice a week at most, but especially after the teaching and application of a new strategy. Be sure to periodically sit with select students to review the forms—to assess the assessing.

3. Many classrooms that buzzed with learning a decade or more ago are essentially buzzless today. High-stakes testing, pacing guides, and scripted learning programs have combined to drain the relevance, engagement, and joy—not to mention complex inquiry and learning—out of hundreds of schools around the country. Kohn (2004, 63) describes—and laments—the situation in similar fashion, stating that "some of the richest learning opportunities are being squeezed out" of the schools.

LEARNING STRATEGY ASSESSMENT

Name_____   Date _____

1. I wanted to learn _____

2. I used the following STRATEGY to help me learn it: (circle <u>one</u>)

- thought about what I know about topic
- got information from pictures/photos
- used other parts of the text to understand new words
- reread difficult parts
- asked myself questions as I read
- predicted as I read
- made pictures in my mind as I read
- asked a peer buddy for help
- used manipulatives, drawings, or a graphic organizer
- other _____

3. This strategy was

very helpful   a little helpful   not helpful

4. Next time, I'm going to try this strategy:

_____

_____

© 2007 by Stephen Cary from *Working with English Language Learners, Second Edition.* Portsmouth, NH: Heinemann.

Figure 8–6.

One of the ways Fiona kept the "learning buzz" going in her classroom was to teach her passions, including airplane design. Her enthusiasm was contagious; students caught the "plane bug" and were off and flying—with content learning, language learning, and with essential how-to-learn strategies.

If your classroom needs a buzz boost, set aside mandated, sleep-inducing curriculum a couple times a week and in its place, substitute activities related to one of your burning passions—gardening, auto mechanics, animated films, cooking, jewelry making, digital photography. If accountability is an issue—"Doing exactly what the state says to do," as one frustrated teacher I recently coached phrased it—choose activities that will develop many of the same concepts and skills purportedly developed by the curriculum piece you're replacing.

9

How do I support a student's first language when I don't speak the language?

READER'S GUIDE
English Language Learner Issue: Primary language support

Key Ideas
- Establish a classroom community that values and celebrates all languages and dialects
- Encourage parents to develop and maintain primary language at home
- Offer primary language support through bilingual parent and community volunteers, peers, cross-age tutors, and extended day programs
- Learn and use some second language yourself with students
- Understand the differences between supporting and developing the primary language

Content:	Newspaper publishing
Grade:	K–1
Teacher Experience:	8 years
ELL Language(s):	Vietnamese, Spanish, Tagalog, Cebuano, Lao, Khmer, Uzbek
School:	K–5, urban

The Classroom Story

Student Language Teachers
School started in less than an hour and Dolores was barely going to make it. Her '87 Saab would be in the repair shop another two or three days and until then, she was dependent on a neighbor friend for transportation.

The friend went through life consistently late and today was no exception. They pulled up in front of Armstrong School with only a few minutes to spare. Dolores gave Gloria a quick thanks for the lift and hurried across the playground to the portables.

Nguyet was waiting at the classroom door. This was a special day for the girl, and her dad had gotten her up early to make sure she was at school before the other kids arrived. Dolores apologized for being late and gave Nguyet a hello hug. A few minutes later, students began trickling into the room.

Nguyet stood beside Dolores at the door and greeted each classmate with a big *Xin chào* (hello) in her best Vietnamese. She was still a little nervous and took the teacher's hand and squeezed hard. The first grader was the only student in Dolores Espinosa's K–1 class who spoke Vietnamese, so she knew she had to get it right. She was this week's language teacher and everybody was counting on her.

Most kids tried to duplicate the Vietnamese in response but were miles off the mark. Nguyet just smiled, kept the greetings coming, and let everyone botch the new language without comment. Even Dolores, who loved language and spent most summers in language-based travel, couldn't quite say it right either, but this was only Monday. Everybody always did better by Friday with the greeting, the "please," and the "thank you."

Dolores planned on having Nguyet teach the class "please" and "thank you" in Vietnamese later in the day, maybe at the cooking center where the kids would fix themselves ants on a log (raisins on peanut butter–filled celery).

Tomorrow, Nguyet's grandmother would be there to teach a song in Vietnamese, the same song kids could hear on tape today at the listening center.

Nguyet was the classroom's sixth language teacher this year. Other students had taught the three-phrase set in Japanese, Spanish, Mandarin, Tagalog, and German. Like Nguyet, each student who wanted would play the language teacher role at some point during the year. Language teachers taught the three phrases informally for a week. Dolores encouraged kids to use the classroom's ever-growing stock of language phrases whenever and wherever they wished. Kids primarily used a phrase set during the week it was introduced, but a few phrases had exceptionally strong legs—like "arigato" and "xiexie," "thank you" in Japanese and Mandarin—and traveled with the students week after week.

Per Dolores' instructions, the classroom language teachers consulted with their parents on which language to teach. Most English learners chose their first language; native English speakers often picked a family heritage language from two, three, or more generations ago. A child's parents or an older brother or sister helped Dolores write out each new phrase set, which was color-coded and then added to butcher paper wall charts. Dolores explained the language teacher component of the program at conference time or during informal parent visits before or after school, always emphasizing how important it was to develop and maintain children's first language on the home front.

After Nguyet's Vietnamese greeting, students settled into their table groups. Dolores provided a quick overview of the day's activities and showed new center material she had scrounged over the weekend—a big box of pipe fittings for the builder center and one of the artifacts for the historian center, this week featuring a 45 rpm record, a hula hoop, and a Hopalong Cassidy lunch box, items kids would discover came from the "ancient" American 1950s.

Jokes for *TAT*

Before center rotation, there was work to do on *The Armstrong Times*, or *TAT*, as most everybody called it. *The Armstrong Times* would never steal subscribers away from *The San Francisco Chronicle*, but it was the only read in town if you were more interested in hamsters than politics. And it was a complete read, too. Where else could the under-eight crowd find a review of a new Saturday morning cartoon show, help for a sick pet, an update on new playground equipment, and a recipe for "Frosted Flake Sandwiches"—all in one place?

Dolores' students published *TAT* every two weeks. This was a publication week and there were a few sections to finish up before the newspaper rolled off the presses (the school copy machine) and "hit the streets."

"We need another joke for the 'Joke Spot,'" Dolores announced, "something good, something really, really funny."

She sat next to a chart paper stand at one end of the classroom, twenty munchkins spread at her feet on the carpet. Each munchkin fanny was planted in a "home square" marked with bright orange tape. A few of the fannies drifted into neighboring territory, but most stayed put.

Kids had collected jokes from family members for last night's homework. Hands shot up, jokes at the ready. Dolores scanned the little faces and smiled. If the kids were crayons, she thought, she'd have every gorgeous color in the box. Students' language riches matched their physical riches; counting English, students spoke eight different languages at home. Four students spoke Spanish as a primary language. Two of the four were Spanish dominant, two were balanced bilinguals, equally comfortable in Spanish and English. Rosita, with Pilipino heritage, was dominant in English, but also spoke Tagalog and Cebuano, as well as some Spanish. Eight students were native English speakers. The remaining seven spoke Lao, Khmer (Cambodian), Vietnamese, and Uzbek, and had beginning to early intermediate English oral skills.

Kids shared their funnies. Some jokes fell flat and others generated a few mild chuckles. The joke that got the biggest laugh would make it into *TAT*. Luis' was a contender: What side of a chicken has the most feathers? Answer: The outside. Christin's joke—What would you have if you put ten ducks in a box? Answer: A box of quackers—was in the running too, but only after Dolores explained the punch line to several students whose ducks did not go "quack" in their first language.

Dolores' personal favorite—You can tune a guitar but you can't tuna fish—offered by Eric and delivered with flawless comic timing, bombed completely. Eric's explanation, a tuna fish can drawing, and a quick tuning demonstration with the class guitar, helped joke comprehension but not joke appreciation; understood or not, the joke was still a loser.

The winning joke—If a rooster was sitting on a fence and laid an egg, which side of the fence would the egg fall on? Answer: Roosters don't lay eggs!—came from Somphavanh who had gotten it from an older brother. The girl told the joke mostly in Lao, with a few words in English provided by a bilingual university volunteer. The volunteer, who helped three days a week for an hour each day, wore a large, laminated paper star pinned to his shirt collar. The star was pale blue with big red letters that said, I KNOW TWO LANGUAGES! Any bilingual parent, community person, or cross-age tutor who worked in the room got to wear a star. Monolingual volunteers wore a star too that read, I CAN HELP!

"OK, good, that takes care of the 'Joke Spot,'" Dolores told the kids, after printing the rooster riddle on chart paper. The university student would later sit with Somphavanh for a few minutes and write the joke out in Lao. Both English and Lao versions would appear in *TAT*.

Dolores read the joke back to Somphavanh and asked her if it was written the way she wanted. Did she use the right words? The girl nodded her head. The teacher then asked the kids to read the joke with her while she tracked the words with a pointer finger. Though Dolores had purposefully written the last word as *egg* instead of *eggs*, all students read the singular form as a plural.

Figure 9–1.

"Hmm, sounds right," mused Dolores, "but I'm not sure if it LOOKS right."

She took a green marker and circled the first *egg*, then asked Alfredo, one of the kinders, to come up and circle other words in the joke that looked the same. Alfredo moved his eyes slowly across and down the text and circled the second *egg* and then the third.

"Good job, Alfredo! You found them all." Alfredo sat down.

Dolores pointed to the last *egg*. "That last *egg* says *egg*, but we need it to say. . . . Let's check." Kids and teacher read the joke one last time.

"Eggs. It needs eggs," said Rosita.

"What will make it say eggs?" asked the teacher. "It's like Spanish, right? Un huevo, dos huevo. . . ."

"Huevos!" Victor shouted, stressing the final consonant.

"Yeah! An *s*," said Dolores, "an *s* for more than one egg."

Dolores added the *s* and ripped off the chart paper and gave it to a volunteer mom, who went to one of the class computers and keyboarded the joke for *TAT*.

"Joke Spot" filled, Dolores distributed rhythm instruments and led everyone through a rousing, high-decibel "If You're Happy and You Know It" (hit your sticks, beat your drum . . .), then through a much softer, but no less fun "El Barquito."

Plumbing Questions

Students moved on to centers. The builder and scientist centers were hooked to the current theme cycle on plumbing. Two weeks ago, Oscar had told about the toilet breaking at his house and about a plumber installing a new one. The toilet story made it into *TAT* and also sparked lots of questions about plumbing, including How long are the pipes? How heavy? Do fish die if they go down the drain? Can you put chicken bones in the garbage disposal? Why does the water taste different at school? Do plumbers ever get trapped under the house? Why does the shower make scary noises?

Dolores and her students would run with the plumbing theme for another week or so until most questions were answered and the theme spark died. They would then move on to another topic of investigation suggested by another student or perhaps by the teacher.

Student-initiated, time-indeterminate theme cycles like those in Dolores' class drove people like Jenny, another K–1 teacher at Armstrong, absolutely crazy. Jenny advertised her program to kids, parents, and administration as an ACADEMIC K–1, and had branded Dolores' class as "loosey-goosey." The loosey-goosey comment and a follow-up declaration that students did not have the luxury of time to pursue answers to "frivolous" questions—like those related to plumbing—had poisoned Jenny's relationship with Dolores. Dolores had not had a kind word to say about Jenny in two years, and vice versa.

At the builder center, kids worked with plastic fittings donated by a parent and explored answers to the question, "What do the pipes look like under the house?" A chart at the center showed L-, T-, and U-shaped pipe configurations. Students constructed the three shapes, then invented a fourth shape they felt could carry and distribute water.

At the scientist center, students tested water collected from classmates' homes to answer the question, "Does water taste better from the kitchen or the bathroom?" A bilingual cross-age tutor helped kids with testing and recording their taste preferences on large graph paper. At one point, the tutor used her Spanish with José Roberto and Yolanda to explain the testing and graphing process. Before returning to her fifth-grade class, the tutor worked a few minutes with the two students in Spanish again, previewing tomorrow's pipe-weighing activity.

In a later rotation at the scientist center, one of the Khmer-English bilingual students translated a buddy's Khmer response for Dolores, who had asked the group about the taste of water at school compared to water at home.

Toward the end of the day, kids sat with the teacher again at the chart stand and completed another item for *TAT*, this time for the "Class News" section. Kids paged through last week's journal entries for possibilities. The journals, five stapled pages filled with drawings and mostly invented spelling text, always provided good material for *TAT*.

After a little discussion, kids decided to report on the tower activity. Students had built the highest towers they could out of half-gallon milk cartons and tape, then measured them using one of their classmate's arms as the standard unit of measure. The tallest tower reached a little over four "Annies." Nicholas dictated his tower journal entry to Dolores who, like before, copied the words onto chart paper. Other students made a few additions and deletions to the text, some offering changes in their first language and bridging to the teacher through a quick English translation provided by other students. The finished text and a companion tower picture copied from a student journal would appear as the lead story in Friday's *TAT* edition.

After school, a few of the kids headed across campus for the extended day program where teachers and parent volunteers conducted some of the activities in Spanish and Vietnamese. Dolores walked to the office, checked her mailbox, and found a message called in earlier from her neighbor friend. The friend would not be able to pick her up till 6:30 or 7:00 tonight and hoped she could find another way home.

Jenny came in and breezed past Dolores and fished out her mail. Neither woman spoke. Dolores remembered that Jenny lived about four blocks from her, but "Ms. Loosey-Goosey" wasn't about to ask for a ride.

Reflections

First Language Support Versus Development

Over coffee in the teacher's lounge, Dolores and I got to talking about our mutual enthusiasm for language diversity and our great disappointment over the passage of Prop. 227, the California anti-bilingual education initiative. We both knew what years of research had shown: Students who develop a strong foundation in their primary language in multiyeared bilingual programs consistently outperform second language learners in all English programs (Krashen and Biber 1988; Ramirez 1991; Krashen 1996; Thomas and Collier 2002; Rolstad, Mahoney, and Glass 2005; Krashen and McField 2005; Slavin and Cheung 2005). Beyond the academic benefits, good bilingual programs also provided students with a clear economic advantage: proficient bilinguals were the "prize hires" in an increasingly competitive global marketplace. Developing the primary language rather than simply supporting it was key in such programs. Support was sporadic and short-term; development was consistent and long-term, and built robust oral and literacy skills in the first language.

But Dolores was a realist. With or without Prop. 227, she could advocate for bilingual education, which she did at every turn, she told me, but she could not unilaterally make it happen for kids. She was still a far cry from reaching Spanish fluency, in spite of several summer excursions to Mexico and Guatemala. Moreover, she was teaching in a district that had run politically hot and cold on bilingual education for years, mainly cold. Prop. 227 made chilly weather even more likely. Finally, she was teaching in a multilingual rather than a bilingual setting. Dolores could support a student's primary language, but she couldn't develop it. But support, she reasoned, was far superior to leaving kids linguistically high and dry. Supports took a variety of forms, from indirect supports like the language teacher role and Dolores' primary language advocacy to parents, to more direct help for kids from bilingual cross-age tutors and volunteers.

As a student language teacher, Nguyet saw her home language sanctioned and thus honored. Because Vietnamese was honored and because Nguyet and all of us have so much of our identity tied to what we speak and how we speak it, honoring Vietnamese honored and validated Nguyet, boosting her feelings of self-worth and empowering her to succeed academically (Cummins 2001).

Carving out class time for learning phrase sets in languages other than English helped Dolores "institutionalize" bilingualism and multilingualism in the classroom. All languages and dialects were found worthy and merited the official seal of approval—at least in Room 2 at Armstrong School. Getting a similar seal of approval from the district, the state of California, and beyond would take a little more time.

Parents as Key Players

Dolores' vision of English learner parents and the role they could play in their children's lives also conflicted with how many others in and out of the district saw the same parents. For Dolores, parents were an invaluable language resource, not just for their own kids, but for other kids in the classroom. She continually invited, cajoled, and sometimes just plain begged parents to help develop primary language at home and at school. On the homefront, parents were encouraged to read and tell stories in the primary language—to keep the home language "burning bright."

At school, direct support from parents included using their primary language skills for oral and written translation, concept explanations, and occasional activity previews and reviews. Twice a year, Dolores offered parents and prospective parent volunteers a two-hour session on how to support the school program at home and how to best help in the classroom. She also invited parents—and grandparents in Nguyet's case—to step out of the traditional helper role whenever they felt comfortable and teach something to the class in their primary language. At least once a month, parents taught a poem or song, told a story, or did a show-and-tell related to a hobby or their work. Dolores encouraged all parents to use movement and as many objects and visuals as they could to make their presentations understandable to kids for whom Spanish, Khmer, or Uzbek, for example, was a new language.

Parent presentations provided primary language academic content for some of the kids while offering native English speakers a chance to learn a little second language. The presentations also gave native English-speaking kids a taste of what their second language learner classmates experienced daily: the periodic fatigue and frustration that comes from trying to learn in a new and sometimes incomprehensible language. That taste of "minority language status" made all kids in Dolores' class second language learners and helped English-only students better appreciate the struggles and accomplishments of their less English-proficient peers.

Like the parent volunteers, bilingual peers, cross-age tutors, and the visiting university student served as "on call" primary language supports. With twenty kids, Dolores could never provide all the one-on-one help she wanted to provide. By necessity, there needed to be more than one teacher in the room most of the time. But more important than the numbers issue was the language issue. Even if she managed to go one-on-one with everyone, she still would have been ineffective with a number of students. Dolores could say "good morning," "please," and "thank you" in a dozen and a half languages at this point but—other than in Spanish—she could not understand extended conversation, field a question, or clarify a difficult concept in any of them. For that, she needed bilingual helpers.

I can't remember seeing another teacher like Dolores who had so many helpers on a regular basis—and this from a guy who's been going into lots of classrooms for lots of years. There were times, of course, when it was Dolores and the twenty kiddos alone and she simply made do, like thousands and thousands of other teachers across the country and the world. But most days, there were several other people in the room students could turn to for primary language help. It was common to see one or two cross-age tutors, a university student, and a volunteer mom or dad in the room at the same time. That changed the teacher-student ratio from one helper for every twenty kids to one helper for every four or five—especially good odds if you're an English learner who's a little shaky on what to do with the Hopalong Cassidy lunch box (guess how old it is). Even with those improved odds, not all kids got the help they needed in their first language—but many got *some* help, and for those students, bilingual helpers made a significant difference.

Dolores had a lot of helpers in the room because she worked hard at getting and keeping all those helpers helping—with phone calls, letters, announcements in *TAT*, the volunteer star pins, and an end-of-the-year appreciation lunch. She was also comfortable with other parents and adults in the room, unlike some teachers who feel compelled to do it all alone—scrape the barnacles, load the cargo, unfurl the sails, and captain the ship from port to port.

TAT and Jokes

Student-generated print surrounded the kids—on the walls, hanging from the ceiling, at the centers, and in the housekeeping, store, and library areas. But it was the classic print-rich environment with a twist—a multilingual print-rich environment. Dolores wanted students to see their language at school, not just hear it. *TAT*, the student newspaper, offered another place for some primary language writing.

TAT also offered a place for jokes. Humor presents a special challenge for second language learners. Even students operating at intermediate to advanced proficiency levels—students with excellent listening comprehension skills and a relatively hefty vocabulary—often struggle with jokes in their second language (Peterson 2001; Schmitz 2002; Cary 2004). Understanding the joke and "getting" the punch line can be tough going. Consider one of the other jokes shared in Dolores' class: What do frogs like to drink? Answer: Croak-a-Cola. Assuming students comprehend all the "surface" vocabulary used in the joke and can discriminate, for example, between the sounds that make up "croak" and those that make up "coke," students must also know that

1. The question is a joke question, not a serious question.
2. The person is setting up a joke structure (riddle question-response).
3. Frogs make a sound called *a croak*.
4. "Drink" can indicate liquid in general or a specific brand of drink.
5. Coca-Cola® is a drink; Croak-a-Cola is not a drink.
6. Frogs don't drink Coca-Cola; if frogs did drink Coca-Cola, it would be odd and funny.
7. *Croak* and *Coke* are similar in sound.
8. The joke (a pun) is in the play on words, *croak* and *Coke*.

So much of the additional knowledge needed to understand the joke is culturally bound. English language learners with limited time in the U.S. will have a difficult time understanding the frog joke—and hundreds of other jokes as well. My hat is off to Dolores and any other teacher willing to tackle jokes in a multilingual setting with a large number of second language kids. Building joke understanding means pulling out all the strategy/technique stops, including using objects, movement, mime, drawing, rephrasing, and the primary language. Dolores pulled all these out and more till most students "got" the jokes.

Language Loss and Recovery

Dolores was a second language learner too, and made sure students saw her as such, using her budding Spanish and trying out each new phrase taught by the language teachers. She worked long and hard in developing and maintaining a classroom culture that not only celebrated languages, but gave students room to try them on for size. Everybody, including the teacher, played with language, risked with language, and made their natural share of errors as they grew with language. Rather than a source for mocking laughter or putdowns, language differences and second language errors were simply a natural part of the linguistic landscape.

Toward the end of our second cup of lounge coffee, I learned why Dolores was so passionate about accepting and nurturing primary language. Her parents had been born in Mexico and entered the American school system without a word of English. Both had been repeatedly punished in Texas with "Spanish Detention"—kept after school for speaking their native language anywhere on the school grounds. The practice continued in the state into the late 1960s (Crawford 2004). Not wanting

Dolores to experience the same sort of humiliation, the parents shielded her from Spanish and emphasized English. It would take several more years of Spanish study for her to recover her lost linguistic heritage. Full recovery, full bilingualism might always elude her. None of her school kids would share a similar language fate if she could help it.

As to Jenny and the "loosey-goosey" slur: Dolores ran one of the most carefully planned, creatively executed, and academically rich K–1 programs I've ever come across. Dolores was about as "loosey-goosey" as Itzhak Perlman navigating a Bach violin concerto.

Discussion and Application

Discussion

1. Primary language support and development programs are often confused, since both include the use of a student's mother tongue. The difference? Support programs offer limited, short-term help in L1, for example: occasional activity previews in Spanish by a bilingual instructional aide, oral summaries of a read-aloud book in Vietnamese by a bilingual parent volunteer, or translation of questions and comments of a Lao-only speaking student by a bilingual classmate. Support programs transition students to all-English instruction as soon as possible. The ultimate goal: English monolingualism, or at best, partial bilingualism—strong English skills with far weaker skills in the mother tongue.

Development programs, on the other hand, provide comprehensive, long-term instruction in the primary language as part of an officially designated bilingual program. Development programs use two languages as media of instruction, teaching academic content and literacy in English and Mandarin, for example. The ultimate goal: bilingualism with strong listening, speaking, reading, and writing skills in both languages.

Since as educators we tend to get what we actively plan and work for, the difference in goals is significant. Though primary language support helps students access core curriculum and is clearly better than no L1 support at all, well-designed, multiyear bilingual programs offer greater academic benefits in content learning and English acquisition. (See top of p. 138 for research citations.)

Consider how, how much, and how long your school includes ELL students' primary languages. To what degree are you supporting or developing first languages? Mark an X where your school falls on the Primary Language Support-Development Continuum (Figure 9–2). If you're not

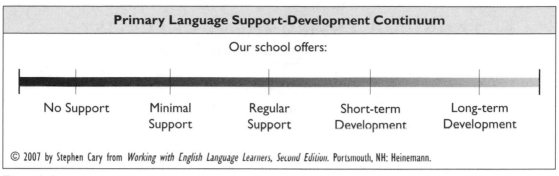

Figure 9-2.

supporting L1, or supporting rather than developing it, what accounts for the choice? Too few second language learners? A lack of funding, human resources, political will? Inadequate information—or misinformation—regarding the benefits and research base for L1 support and development?

Some schools support or develop L1 for their largest population of English learners, say Spanish speakers, but offer only spotty support for their pocket language students—students from school groups with very few speakers, perhaps Khmer, Uzbek, or Somali. If you've got pocket language students needing additional help in L1, what school, parent, and community resources could you bring to bear to increase the level of support?

2. A school's mix of programs, policies, procedures, and attitudes related to languages other than English determines its overall language atmosphere or environment. Welcoming environments value and promote the use of students' primary languages; hostile environments discourage or prohibit their use. Teachers and administrators at Dolores' school were intent on establishing and maintaining a positive, welcoming language environment for second language learners.

Reflect on your own school's language atmosphere, using the Language Environment Checklist (Figure 9–3) as a guide. More "yes" answers indicate a more positive environment; more "no" answers, a more negative environment. What can you and colleagues do to turn negatives into positives and improve the language environment?

3. As the number of English learners continues to rise throughout the country, I'm finding more and more teachers who are second language

LANGUAGE ENVIRONMENT CHECKLIST
LOTE = languages other than English

	Yes	No
1. ELL students use LOTE freely in and out of class, without fear of putdowns by peers or teachers.		
2. Support (or development) in LOTE is provided by bilingual teachers, aides, volunteers, or cross-age tutors.		
3. Materials in LOTE are available in classrooms and the library/media center.		
4. Stated and unstated school policies encourage the use of LOTE at school.		
5. Parents are encouraged to develop LOTE at home.		
6. Most staff view the use of LOTE at school in positive terms.		
7. Most native English-speaking students view the use of LOTE at school in positive terms.		
8. Student work in LOTE is displayed in classrooms, hallways, and on school/class websites.		
9. School provides bilingual interpreters at events, governance meetings, and parent-teacher conferences.		
10. School uses LOTE in written communication with parents/community.		

Figure 9-3.

learners themselves—making time in their busy schedules to learn Spanish, Vietnamese, Hmong, Mandarin, Arabic, Russian, or any one of a hundred other languages. Knowing even a minimal amount of a student's L1—perhaps basic greetings and "please" and "thank you"—helps a teacher create a more nurturing classroom atmosphere, honor and validate all languages and dialects, and promote bilingualism and multiculturalism at school and beyond. A simple "buenos días" or "gracias," for example, sends a loud and unambiguous signal to your newly arrived Spanish-speaking student: I'm interested in your language, in your culture, in you.

Teachers with moderate to larger amounts of a second language can use it to periodically help students understand a difficult concept or conduct parts of a parent-teacher conference or home visit in the primary language.

Using a five-level scale—beginning, early intermediate, intermediate, early advanced, advanced—how would you rate yourself on second language development? Assuming you haven't reached an advanced, native-speaking level in your L2, what's your plan of action for continued growth?

I'm an intermediate-level Spanish speaker and when I promote bilingualism in teacher workshops, I'm frequently asked about my own plan for maintaining (and hopefully!) boosting Spanish skills. In addition to spending a couple weeks in Mexico each summer working on a social project, I periodically:

- use Spanish with students in the public schools
- socialize with Spanish-speaking friends
- listen to favorite Spanish-speaking singers
- watch films in Spanish
- write emails in Spanish
- read online news and comics in Spanish

Comics, in particular, have been a rich source of learning for me—and for many students and teachers I work with. For comics resources in multiple languages and ideas on how to use these powerful tools for L2 building in the classroom, see Cary (2004).

Obviously, your L2 acquisition plan will vary according to individual need, interest level, learning style, and available time. The key is to have a plan!

Application

1. Consider the ways Dolores supported primary language:

- personally learning/using some L1 of her students
- having students serve as L1 "language teachers"

- inviting parents to guest teach in L1
- using university/parent volunteers, peer and cross-age tutors for
    L1 concept explanations, activity previews and reviews
- including L1 content in *TAT* (official multilingual publication)
- displaying student work in all languages
- honoring bilingual skills with I KNOW TWO LANGUAGES! badges
- encouraging students to attend an extended day program for
    L1 help
- encouraging parents to maintain/develop L1 at home

Choose one or two items from the above list that would be workable in your classroom and implement.

2. Watching students struggle to understand jokes in Dolores' class reminds us how elusive humor can be in a second language. Moreover, students who consistently miss or misinterpret jokes can easily feel frustrated and isolated since humor is one of the significant ways to "get solid" with one's peer group. Dolores understood the key role humor plays in students' emotional-social lives. She also knew that most students find jokes inherently fun and interesting and are therefore ideal hooks for developing L2 language and L2 cultural knowledge. She felt spending classroom time on joke "making and getting" was more than justified; it was essential. To help your second language learners with joke "making and getting," try one or more of the following:

1. Schedule time slots, say two fifteen-minute sessions per week, for students to tell and explain jokes and humorous anecdotes.
2. Take time to briefly explain jokes and puns that surface during regular instruction/activities.
3. Create an ever-expanding joke book that circulates through the class with students reading the latest jokes and adding their own. Students with low literacy skills can audio record their jokes or share them via student-to-teacher dictation.
4. Have students periodically include cartoons, comic strips, jokes, and funny stories in their journals.
5. Work on humor while honoring and supporting L1 at the same time by comparing and contrasting jokes across languages. Students and teachers alike find it fascinating why the same joke is hilarious in one language/cultural setting and a total dud in another.

3. How important are bilingual volunteers for primary language support? At many schools around the country, especially those with a new population of English learners or those with very small numbers of speakers of various languages, the answer is a definitive: absolutely critical. These schools often lack paid bilingual staff and may also lack the funding, time, or political will to hire and train bilingual staff. In these settings, volunteers mean the difference between some L1 support and no support.

If you're in such a school and want some primary language help for your students on core curriculum concepts, start a bilingual volunteer program, preferably with the help (and blessing) of principal, colleagues, and site council. Sources for volunteers include:

- parents and extended family members
- colleges and universities (international students)
- churches, synagoges, mosques, and temples
- large local employers
- social service clubs
- senior centers
- community centers

Two important hints: One, most volunteer programs will quickly fall apart without someone on staff taking on the responsibility of volunteer coordinator. Two, always make your volunteers feel needed and valued!

10

How do I minimize communication conflicts in a multilingual classroom?

READER'S GUIDE

English Language Learner Issue: Cross-cultural/communication conflict

Key Ideas
- Establish a classroom community that values and celebrates diversity
- Seek out and exploit student common ground
- Provide frequent opportunities for meaningful collaborative work
- Emphasize "doing" over "telling" solutions
- See conflicts as inevitable but solvable given critical reflection and persistence

Content:	Visual arts
Grade:	6–8
Teacher Experience:	17 years
ELL Language(s):	Cantonese, Spanish, Japanese, Arabic
School:	Middle school, urban

The Classroom Story

Words as Weapons

The teacher let the words slip by the first time, wanting to give Hector the benefit of the doubt. The remark came as he modeled a cartooning technique for some students on the other side of the room. Toby hoped he had misunderstood the boy's words. But here they were again, directed to Jin Ye, louder, and this time unmistakable: "Chopstick Boy!" Hector reinforced the slur with a mocking laugh. Jin Ye shot a hand across the table and snatched Hector's comic strip and was about to rip it in two when

Toby intervened and took the boys out into the hallway for a quick, impromptu heart-to-heart.

Though rattled by the slur, Toby had half expected it. There had been a series of other troubling incidents in fifth period during the first and second weeks of school, though nothing as ugly as Hector's verbal slap. Two native speakers had teased ELL students about their English pronunciation and jumbled syntax. Following suit, one of the English learners had belittled native speakers' lack of bilingual skills. Eduardo had interpreted Colin's use of the English idiom "eat your heart out" as an insult and had responded with a string of obscenities in Spanish. Sachie, from Japan, perceived Ehab's physical closeness when talking to her as a sexual advance and had labeled all Palestinian males as "stupid-bad."

Toby wasn't sure if his new middle school job required an art teacher or a UN peace keeping specialist. Art he knew. Toby Overbeek lived and breathed line, form, and color. He had become an art teacher nearly twenty years ago and had doggedly stayed the course. Each time a district suddenly declared art a pricey educational frill and snipped it out of the budget, Toby picked up his paint box and teaching talent and moved on, refusing to trade drawing and sculpture for social studies or PE. Persevering as an art teacher meant changing states twice and districts five times. Given the art boom and bust cycle, Toby understood that tenure would probably always be out of reach.

Though Toby's job hopping had given him experience with a variety of grade levels, programs, and youngsters, this was his first time teaching large numbers of second language learners in a multilingual setting. Nothing had adequately prepared him for fifth period at Hawkins Middle School and what he was secretly referring to as "my own little Balkans."

Each of Toby's classes contained English language learners, with two periods running over 50 percent ELL. Students spoke at least three different primary languages in every class. In fifth period, students spoke five: English, Spanish, Cantonese, Japanese, and Arabic. Many of the students were at a beginning to early intermediate stage of English proficiency.

Toby assumed a certain number of cross-cultural communication problems were simply unavoidable; they came with the territory of the multilingual classroom. Yet the tone and nature of some of the comments, especially Hector's, pointed to something far more serious—simmering racism. The teacher believed a PowerPoint® slide show on the rich variety of art around the world would help reduce such problems, if only slightly. The slides would detail the important contributions of all groups to the aesthetic whole, especially those groups represented in the classroom. Appreciation for a people's art would generalize to an appreciation of the people themselves, or so Toby hoped. And you don't slur people you value.

Yet rather than building an appreciation for diversity, the slides provided some students with the ammunition to denigrate it. Some slides triggered boos and derisive hoots; others brought comments touting the creative superiority of one group over another. Though the majority of students made no disparaging remarks, those who did were able to sabotage the show. Toby wondered about those students who remained silent throughout the slides. How many valued diversity in art and, by logical extension, in humanity, and how many feared it? For how many students had ethnic pride become ethnic hubris? And how many would someday move from hubris to hatred? Was Hector already there? Or was his "Chopstick Boy" comment merely a button pusher, a throwaway, adolescent banter line? Hector had apologized to Jin Ye in the hallway and claimed he was unaware of the force and racist quality of his words, but Toby wasn't sure if this was really the case or not.

The PowerPoint® slide show bombed and so did Toby's suggestion halfway through the week that students sit next to somebody "different" in order to make a new friend. Most students continued to group themselves at the tables in ethnic enclaves, English speakers on the right, Spanish speakers on the left, Cantonese, Japanese, and Arabic speakers in the middle, front to back. Students rarely interacted with those outside their own language group, and what little interaction there was, was again, often strained or discordant.

Comments and reactions during the slides and opening cartooning unit activities indicated that a number of students were looking at art and thinking about art not as art—good or bad, engaging or stupefying—but as Arabic art versus European art, Chicano art versus Japanese art, "my art" versus "your art." Cartooning and the drawings, paintings, sculpture, and craftwork shown in the slides were seen by some students in the same terms as competitive sport. Art was like football or soccer or boxing, something to win rather than something to make.

Week three found Toby holding more hallway heart-to-hearts and preaching several "One People, One Planet" sermonettes to the entire class. Nothing was having much effect. Racially charged comments continued; communication blowups increased. And little was happening on the art learning front. Toby knew he desperately needed to turn things around, and turn them around quickly, but was not at all sure what to try next.

Off the Soapbox

At the start of week four, Toby took the advice of a colleague at Hawkins and stopped preaching to kids about the need to get along and instead gave them a reason to get along—the need to make art together. Students worked in artists' collectives in groups of four to produce works for an online gallery show on Hawkins' website.

Toby composed the collectives with language in mind. Each group contained at least two different primary languages and several had students from three different language backgrounds. Regardless of the mix, Toby made sure every group had at least one student with intermediate- to native-level English language skills. Hector and Jin Ye were placed in the same group, which Toby saw as either an inspired act of management brilliance on his part or absolute stupidity; the boys would either get along or kill each other trying. Some students initially grumbled about having to work with classmates they didn't know or "couldn't understand." Toby dismissed the grumbling and plunged into the projects.

Groups began by choosing a piece of artwork that all members liked—though not necessarily to the same degree—from teacher-supplied magazine pictures of drawings and paintings by artists from around the world. Pictures carried no identifying data. Students used reference books, CD-ROMs, art history websites, and their own prior knowledge to determine the artist, country, period, and stylistic school of their group's chosen piece.

Once the piece was identified, students located other examples by the same artist (or school) and, when possible, from the same time period.

Each collective then generated a list of technical elements that characterized the artist's work. Toby circulated, posed questions, and engaged students in dialogue about what they were seeing in the various works in order to help groups identify key elements. The group that chose a Kandinsky painting as a favorite, for example, characterized his work from around 1910 as having bright colors, floating faces, soft shapes in black outlines, and "colors sticking on top of other colors."

Students then decided on a preferred medium for rendering their projects—colored pencil or watercolors. Each member in a collective was to produce an original work rather than a knockoff copy. Works were to capture the artist's fundamental style, reflecting the key elements that distinguished that style. Members were to collaborate with one another, offering encouragement, technical assistance, and feedback on the inclusion of their artist's style markers. Pieces that incorporated the artist's key elements were eligible for the gallery show; those that didn't, weren't. Everyone in a group got in, or no one did.

The subject matter for the original works was open, with one stipulation: the topic had to be the same for all members in a collective and each member had to have direct, personal experience with the subject. Topics chosen included conflicts with siblings, playing on a soccer team, fear of physical abuse, and pop music stars.

Onto the Web

Throughout the six-week unit, Toby served as "artist in residence." He offered demonstrations and instruction in the two media, spotlighting the techniques employed by groups' favorite artists. Student "apprentices" prepared a small scale mock-up of their proposed piece and had the teacher and their collective buddies check it for key elements. After getting the go-ahead from Toby, groups moved on to the larger-scale works.

As with the mock-ups, members of each collective offered one another help and constructive criticism as the final projects took form. Toby earmarked a few minutes of each period for "feedback time." The degree of collaboration varied widely among students. Some interacted and helped each other regularly, others interacted and helped only with lots of gentle nudging by Toby. Though students still struggled to understand one another's English, they struggled without the complaining, hurtful teasing, and emotional explosions so prevalent in the first two weeks of classes. It looked like Hector and Jin Ye had signed a peace treaty of sorts; they weren't collaborating much, but they were no longer at each other's throat.

In week six, students photographed their completed works, and with the help of the tech lab teacher, transferred the photos to the computer and onto the school's website. Each collective's submittal to the online gallery show included a brief biographical sketch of its artist, a listing of style markers, and a blurb on why the group found this particular artist so appealing. As the gallery show's curator, Toby required each collective to provide written information in English and in all other languages represented in the group. Other works in other media, some done alone and some in reformulated collectives, were added to the gallery as the year progressed.

Conflicts between students in period five continued, but gradually decreased in frequency and intensity. The problems that were coming up in the second semester, Toby noticed, were much more likely to spring from academic or girl-boy raging hormone issues than from language and cultural differences. Most students were getting along and getting the art concepts and skills the teacher was working so hard to deliver.

Students would not need the UN peace keeping specialist after all, Toby decided. A good old art teacher without tenure would do them nicely.

Reflections

Telling Versus Doing Solutions

Communication conflicts, especially those as serious as Toby was experiencing, never have an easy fix. Helping students at any age and from any background treat one another with courtesy, concern, and respect takes some doing, and usually some tough doing. Adding a variety of first languages, second language proficiencies, and cultures into the mix can make the job even tougher. Though diversity in the student population offers the possibility of multiple perspectives on any curriculum topic, and hence, richer learning for all, differences can also increase the chance of misunderstandings between students.

Simple and quite natural misunderstandings based on an inability to comprehend what a classmate is saying or an inability to clearly communicate one's thoughts and feelings sometime spin out of control and turn nasty. Conflicts over home culture values or over something as seemingly innocuous as distance between speakers, in Sachie and Ehab's case, may deflect student attention, disrupt a class, and demolish the most carefully crafted lesson or activity. Finally, and potentially the cause of the gravest conflicts, a few students, like Hector perhaps, will ingest bigotry at home or in the community and spit it back out in the classroom.

Toby walked into a situation where whatever—and whoever—could be in conflict either was or soon would be. Tackling the conflicts head-on with the PowerPoint® slide show, hallway heart-to-hearts, and inspirational sermonettes made sense. The slides told kids that all cultures have artists, all people have the capacity for artistic expression; the heart-to-hearts told kids that Toby cared enough to deal with them as individuals and not embarass them in front of their peers; the sermonettes told the class as a whole where people of good will stood on language and cultural diversity.

But all three were *telling* solutions rather than *doing* solutions, which of course meant they were dead with most middle school youngsters from the word go. Kids were listening to Toby talk about the need to get along, but few were really hearing, taking his words to heart, and modifying behavior. Moreover, ELL students with beginning-level English proficiency found the sermonizing mostly incomprehensible.

The tide turned and communication problems diminished as Toby traded preaching for something he did a whole lot better: making art. The key to the communication improvement hinged on how kids made the art, rather than on the type of art kids made. Students from different language and cultural backgrounds placed in artist's collectives had the opportunity to collaborate. Yet students don't magically start collaborating —especially those with a lousy track record of communicating well with one another. What made collaboration possible, and in fact probable, was having a genuine reason to collaborate. Students needed to pool art and language skills to prepare the best work they could for the online gallery show. The online show was a powerful and seductive hook: Each collective's works would have a real audience, "gallery freaks" in Toby's terms, likely in the hundreds of viewers, but potentially in the tens of millions. There was a point to all the art making beyond a grade: people were really going to look at this stuff!

The promise of big exposure made for big student buy-in, and the buy-in, Toby felt, spurred students on to working harder, learning harder. Communication conflicts were counterproductive to securing a spot in the online gallery show. Getting along as a group would help launch their work into cyberspace; not getting along, not helping each other, not meeting gallery criteria, might mean gallery rejection. Toby's use of a studio art, master-apprentice model provided additional real-world qualities to the unit. The classroom was a production studio for artists rather than simply a place to go for art lessons.

The Language of Art and the Art of Language

The instructional model offered students the chance to build language skills right along with art expertise. ELL students improved their conversational English as they discussed work with the teacher and their groupmates. They improved English reading and writing skills as they researched their artist and prepared reports for gallery submittals. Interwoven throughout the oral and literacy work was academic language, in this case the language of the visual arts—the language of art history, art production, and art criticism. Structured feedback time gradually moved from a rough and stilted exercise to an authentic give-and-take between students. Toby's "master artist" demos, question posing, and ongoing dialogues showed students not only what to talk about in art (the essential vocabulary), but how to talk about it as well (the essential language structures and conventions).

In and out of artist collectives, the rule is one artist per pencil drawing or watercolor painting. So, thank heavens, Toby did not have collective members go a one-piece and four-artist route for the sake of group solidarity and communication conflict reduction. Not only would the route have broken with real-world art making, it may have easily increased student friction, as in, "Paint wings on my cow and you're dead meat!" What *did* help students make friends and curb antagonisms was the need for each person's work in the collective to relate to the same basic life experience. As students talked with one another and searched for a significant common experience, they learned about each other's background, likes, dislikes, fears, and hopes. Without Toby or anyone else having to preach it, students soon discovered one of the foundation truths in any good multicultural education or conflict management program: Our differences are intriguing, but what is just as interesting and finally more important, is how much more alike we are than different.

The need to get the job done—to find the topic, complete the artwork, and get online!—required good communication between students. And good communication meant that collective members had to listen to one another, to make sense of each other's words, to do whatever was necessary to get their message across. Students used dictionaries and pantomime, rephrased misunderstood statements and questions, and often called on someone with bilingual skills to help clear the static and keep the lines of communication open. Students saw the importance of bilingual skills again as they prepared written information to accompany their gallery pieces. Each additional language used increased a group's potential audience. More languages, more hits.

After the first few weeks of "communication wars" and failed pep talks, Toby told me he had rethought his management goals for fifth period. He was now after a slow-growth improvement in student-to-student communication rather than a total end to hostilities and instant, happy-face pluralism. Toby got what he was after. By the end of the six-week unit, cross-cultural conflicts had decreased substantially. Students—certainly not all, but many more than before—were giving each other some slack and some consideration as they all wrestled with the tricky business of communicating in a multilingual and "multicustomed" setting. Communication blowups were rarely getting in the way of making art. And Hector and Jin Ye had not killed each other.

Conflicts with Parents

Though Toby was dealing with more than his fair share of student-student friction, conflicts with parents were nonexistent. Knock on wood. Parent-teacher conflicts can be as difficult to manage and resolve as classroom conflicts.

Two examples from Cole Elementary, one of the feeder schools into Hawkins, show how sparks can fly when home and school values collide. Like most K and K–1 rooms in the U.S., each of the three kindergartens at Cole has a housekeeping center, where kids play at cooking, cleaning, and parenting. One immigrant dad from Mexico with a son in one of the K rooms asked his boy's teacher to prohibit the child from going into the housekeeping area. The dad felt that domestic play was inappropriate for his son and, in fact, for all boys. Through a bilingual community liaison, the teacher made it clear that she could not honor such a request since all activities in the room were open to both girls and boys. Educational equity required equal access, the teacher gently explained. Two more parent-teacher talks followed, each ending with an emotionally exhausted teacher and a disappointed and angry dad.

Another dad, from Pakistan, asked his daughter's fifth-grade teacher at Cole to make sure the girl was never seated next to a boy. The dad was intent on short-circuiting any possible romantic involvements. In the same gentle and respectful manner used by the K teacher, the fifth-grade teacher explained to the dad that such a seating arrangement would be impossible to implement. All students needed to learn from one another and needed to learn to work together across ethnic and gender lines. Again: another unhappy and upset father and multiple parent-teacher meetings.

In both examples, each dad had strong, culturally based, heart-felt concerns. So did the teachers. In the end, there were no perfect, everybody-wins-big solutions. But there *were* solutions, based on compromise, and therefore acceptable to all parties: The K teacher would not prohibit the boy from entering the housekeeping center, but neither would she encourage the boy to play there. The fifth-grade teacher would not seat the daughter permanently next to a boy, but the girl would periodically interact with boys in pair and small group activities. As with Toby, a respect for cultural differences and some critical reflection and persistence enabled the Cole teachers to ultimately fashion workable solutions.

Postscript

A final note on the Hawkins' gallery show, after six months online: nearly 3,200 hits and counting. Not bad for student art. I say give Toby tenure and let the poor guy unpack his bags.

Discussion and Application

Discussion

1. Cross-cultural conflicts can arise between students, students and teachers, or parents and teachers. Moreover, they come in all shapes and sizes, from minor, short-lived problems over a mispronounced or misunderstood word in the second language, to major, continuing blowups over real or perceived racism. Use the checklist (Figure 10–1) to reflect on the types of conflicts in your classroom or school.

CONFLICT CHECKLIST

Put a check mark beside each item that regularly generates conflicts.

_____ inadequate knowledge (about cultural groups)

_____ customs/values (for example, gender roles)

_____ name calling/put-downs (racial/ethnic slurs)

_____ oral communication (misinterpretation, teasing)

_____ facial expressions, body language (misinterpretation)

_____ proxemics (distance between speakers)

_____ touching behavior (appropriate vs. inappropriate)

_____ parent-school expectations

_____ other _____

_____ other _____

Figure 10-1.

2. Synthesize the information generated above, and place an an X on the continuum in Figure 10–2 to indicate an overall level of cross-cultural conflict. A "1" means a classroom or school with minor, infrequent, and resolvable cross-cultural problems. Disruptions are few and psychological or physical hurt to students is rare. Peace between groups is the norm. A "5" means a classroom or school with major, frequent, and seemingly intractable cross-cultural problems. Disruptions are many and psychological or physical hurt to students is routine. Hostility between groups is the norm. Compare your present level of conflict with that of two or three years ago. Has the number and severity of conflicts increased, decreased, or stayed about the same? What might account for the change, if any?

3. Toby eventually—and wisely—turned to projects done in artist collectives as a way to deal with cross-cultural conflict. Research shows that beyond the boost in academic achievement, collaborative (aka, cooperative) learning can significantly reduce prejudice and classroom conflict (Johnson and Johnson 1995; Slavin 2001; Nieto 2004). Some keys to successful collaborative groups: teacher modeling, ethnic/language diversity, equal-status interactions via role rotation, and tasks that require students to mutually support and depend on one another.

Consider your own use of collaborative learning structures. How often are students placed in ethnically and linguistically diverse groups where—to get the job done—they must talk together, plan together, work together? Daily? A couple times a week? Rarely? When you use collaborative, hetereogeneous structures, how would you rate their effectiveness for helping students learn target concepts and skills? For reducing or eliminating cross-cultural friction in the classroom?

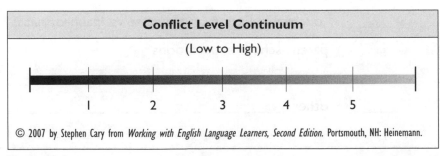

Figure 10-2.

Application

1. Teachers who have taught in both monolingual and multilingual settings frequently tell me they prefer a multilingual classroom—even with its inescapable and often thorny cross-cultural conflicts. Why? They know a multilingual classroom offers students (and teachers) a golden opportunity to:

- reduce stereotyping, racism, linguicism, ethnocentrism
- become comfortable with diversity
- learn about other cultures
- learn elements of a second (or third or fourth!) language
- see the world through different eyes
- build cross-cultural friendships

Golden opportunities, however, as Toby discovered, can be tarnished and lost altogether if cross-cultural conflicts aren't dealt with promptly and appropriately. And that takes lots of good strategies.

Alone, with a colleague, or as a faculty, consider the strategies you're presently using to minimize and resolve conflicts in your classroom and school. Divide a piece of paper into three columns. In the first column, list the strategies. In the second, put a *T* or a *D* beside each strategy to indicate whether it's a "telling" or "doing" type solution. In the last column, place a double plus sign (++) if the strategy is consistently effective, a single plus sign (+) if sometimes effective, and a minus (−) if consistently ineffective. Review the data. If you have

- too few total strategies
- too narrow a range of strategy types
- too few "doing" solutions
- too few consistently effective strategies

rethink and revamp your classroom or school-wide plan for dealing with cross-cultural conflicts.

2. Teachers must often tackle cross-cultural conflicts on-the-fly, with little or no previous experience with the target issue to help them resolve the situation. A conflict erupts, and for the physical and psychological safety of students, we act. Though nothing beats experience as a guide, we can increase our chances for successful conflict resolution by imagining specific conflicts before they arise and brainstorming possible solutions.

Working with a colleague (or faculty group), develop an ethical, efficient, and effective solution for each cross-cultural conflict listed below. The sample conflicts—all sticky, all potentially serious—come from teachers I've coached over the past several years. As you fashion solutions, consider both action and prevention. What would you do to resolve each conflict, and what could you do to minimize the chance of the conflict occurring in the first place? Add other school-specific conflicts to the list if needed.

Grades K–2
- A girl from Cambodia starts crying after a classmate mocks her "bad English."
- Older students yell "wetback" at a first grader from Mexico as he walks to school each day.
- A teacher repeatedly orders a soft-spoken boy from Thailand to "Speak up!" The boy becomes even quieter and soon stops offering opinions in class.
- A teacher mentions at a faculty meeting that her Kinders from Mexico started the school year with "hardly any language—English *or* Spanish" and that the "little Spanish" they speak is an "off brand" variety. Sparks fly between the teacher and several colleagues.

Grades 3–5
- Classmates label a Korean-speaking student "stupid" because of his frequent mispronunciations and jumbled syntax.
- Two brothers from Jordan are repeatedly called "terrorists" by kids on the playground.
- A teacher believes her Taiwanese student might be guilty because he avoids eye contact when questioned about a stolen backpack.
- Mexican heritage parents perceive their daughter's teacher as cold and rude after she refuses a drink and a snack during a home visit.

Grades 6–8
- A Laotian girl feels humiliated after a classmate asks if houses have bathrooms in her home country.
- Two native English speakers tell the teacher they won't do group work with "illegal alien" kids.
- An ELD teacher finds that several hand gestures she commonly uses—OK, thumbs up, and calling people to the front of the class

with an upturned finger—are considered rude or obscene by some of her new immigrant students.

- A teacher concerned by the "overly huggy" behavior of his Latino students establishes a "no-hug" policy.

Grades 9–12

- An Iranian girl's hijab (head scarf) is yanked and nearly pulled off by a classmate who shouts, "Dress like an American!"
- A girl from El Salvador misses at least three school days a month to care for her baby brother.
- A boy from Somalia interprets a classmate's well-intentioned, "You're my homey!" as a derogatory comment.
- Through a translator, parents from Taiwan express their dismay over a school counselor's comment that their son "should make his own career decision."
- The mother of an Indonesian girl is furious with teachers for allowing a boy to pat her daughter on the back and shoulders.

3. Collaborative, project-based "doing" solutions to cross-cultural conflict take time to plan and implement. It's a lot easier and a lot faster to tell students to "make nice" or cite the consequences for breaking school rules. Toby's "telling" solutions—encouraging cross-cultural friendships, hallway heart-to-hearts, and the let's-all-get-along sermonettes—were quick, but highly ineffective. Artist collectives took triple the time, but eventually paid off in conflict reduction.

If you're dealing with mild to serious cross-cultural discord in your classroom, try a collaborative "doing" project as a way to diminish conflict—and learn content. Take cues from Toby: Use culturally and linguistically diverse groups, high-interest subject matter, and keep the groups together for a minimum of four to six weeks. Be sure to choose a project that requires frequent and extensive cooperation among group members to complete.

Epilogue

Question Eleven

Two days after finishing the book, Question Eleven rolled in. I knew it was just a matter of time before somebody asked a burning question that didn't make the cut, but Question Eleven's early arrival caught me by surprise.

I was working with a small group of teachers whose first few questions about English language learners came right out of the Top Ten. I mentioned the upcoming book and how I wished we had it in hand so we could read through one or two of the classroom stories. The stories would provide some strategy ideas and give us more grist for the teacher reflection mill.

The group expressed enthusiasm for the book and wished me well on the project, then popped dreaded number eleven. One of the teachers hoped the Top Ten included a question on evaluating commercial ELD materials. I said I thought that was a great question, but unfortunately, with space and time limitations, I had to make some tough decisions on what got in and what didn't. Sorry.

The woman let out a small sigh of disappointment and my spirits sank. To make matters worse, Question Twelve came on the heels of Eleven. Another teacher wondered if I had a question dealing with ELD and primary language literacy programs for parents. She and her school desperately needed some good information on those topics. Would the book help? Again, I had to say I was sorry and refer her to other sources. Thank heavens the next question was a carbon copy of a Top Ten item. My spirits scrambled out of the basement and back into the sunshine.

I know every reader has another burning question that didn't make the Top Ten. But my hope is that the book provided you with some answers, if only tentative, to several of your other questions, and some resources for helping you answer your own Question Eleven and beyond. If so, I can stay where it's sunny.

References

Ada, A. F. 1988. "The Pajaro Valley Experience: Working with Spanish-Speaking Parents to Develop Children's Reading and Writing Skills in the Home through the Use of Children's Literature." In *Minority Education: From Shame to Struggle*, pp. 223–38. Edited by T. Skutnabb-Kangas and J. Cummins. Clevedon, England: Multilingual Matters.

Artiles, A. J., and A. A. Ortiz, eds. 2002. *English Language Learners with Special Education Needs: Identification, Assessment, and Instruction*. McHenry, IL: Delta Systems/Center for Applied Linguistics.

Asher, J. 1977. *Learning Another Language Through Actions: The Complete Teacher's Guidebook*. Los Gatos, CA: Sky Oaks Productions.

Bliatout, B. T., B. T. Downing, J. Lewis, and D. Yang. 1988. *Handbook for Teaching Hmong-Speaking Students*. Sacramento, CA: Folsom Cordova Unified School District, Southeast Asia Community Resource Center. Entire handbook available online at: http://www.seacrc.org/media/pdfiles/HmongBk.pdf.

Brinton, D., and P. Master, eds. 1997. *New Ways in Content-Based Instruction*. Alexandria, VA: TESOL.

Brown, H. D. 2007. *Principles of Language Learning and Teaching*. 5th ed. White Plains, NY: Pearson/Longman.

California Department of Education. 2006. Student demographics (English Learners). Available online at: http//dq.cde.ca.gov/dataquest/.

Carrier, K. A. 2003. "Improving High School English Language Learners' Second Language Listening Through Strategy Instruction." *Bilingual Research Journal* 27: 383–408.

Cary, S. 1998. The Effectiveness of a Contextualized Storytelling Approach for Second Language Acquisition. Doctoral dissertation, University of San Francisco, San Francisco, CA.

———. 2004. *Going Graphic: Comics at Work in the Multilingual Classroom*. Portsmouth, NH: Heinemann.

Chamot, A. U. 2005. "Language Learning Strategy Instruction: Current Issues and Research." *Annual Review of Applied Linguistics* 25: 112-30.

Chamot, A. U., and J. M. O'Malley. 1994. *The Calla Handbook: Implementing the Cognitive Academic Language Learning Approach.* Reading, MA: Addison-Wesley.

———. 1996. "The Cognitive Academic Language Learning Approach: A Model for Linguistically Diverse Classrooms." *Elementary School Journal* 96 (3): 259–73.

Cortés, C. E. 1986. "The Education of Language Minority Students: A Contextual Interaction Model." In *Beyond Language: Social and Cultural Factors in Schooling Language Minority Students,* pp. 3–33. Edited by D. Holt. Los Angeles: California State University Evaluation, Dissemination, and Assessment Center.

Crawford, J. 2004. *Educating English Learners: Language Diversity in the Classroom.* 5th ed. (Formerly, *Bilingual Education: History, Politics, Theory, and Practice.*) Los Angeles: Bilingual Educational Services, Inc.

Cummins, J. 2001. *Negotiating Identities: Education for Empowerment in a Diverse Society.* 2d ed. Los Angeles: California Association for Bilingual Education.

Díaz-Rico, L. T., and K. Z. Weed. 2006. *The Crosscultural, Language, and Academic Development Handbook: A Complete K–12 Reference Guide.* 3d ed. Boston: Pearson Education, Inc.

Doughty, C. 2003. "Instructed SLA: Constraints, Compensation, and Enhancement." In *The Handbook of Second Language Acquisition,* pp. 256–310. Edited by C. Doughty and M. Long. Malden, MA: Blackwell Publishing.

Dragan, P. B. 2005. *A How-To Guide for Teaching English Language Learners in the Primary Classroom.* Portsmouth, NH: Heinemann.

Dye, G. 2002. "Language Learning in the American Southwestern Borderlands: Navajo Speakers and Their Transition to Academic English Literacy." *Bilingual Research Journal* 26 (3): 611–30.

Echevarria, J., M. Vogt, and D. J. Short. 2004. *Making Content Comprehensible for English Language Learners: The SIOP Model.* 2d ed. Boston: Allyn and Bacon.

Ellis, R. 1986. *Understanding Second Language Acquisition.* Oxford: Oxford University Press.

Foster, P., and P. Skehan. 1996. "The Influence of Planning and Task Type on Second Language Performance." *Studies in Second Language Acquisition* 18: 299–323.

Freeman, Y. S., and D. E. Freeman. 1998. *ESL/EFL Teaching: Principles for Success*. Portsmouth, NH: Heinemann.

Freire, P. 1970. *Pedagogy of the Oppressed*. New York: The Continuum Publishing Company.

Garan, E. M. 2002. *Resisting Reading Mandates: How to Triumph with the Truth*. Portsmouth, NH: Heinemann.

Goodman, K. S. 1996. *On Reading*. Portsmouth, NH: Heinemann.

Gottlieb, M. 1995. "Nurturing Student Learning Through Portfolios." *TESOL Journal* 5 (1): 12–14.

Graves, D. 2003. *Writing: Teachers and Children at Work*. Portsmouth, NH: Heinemann.

Harste, J., V. Woodward, and C. Burke. 1984. *Language Stories and Literacy Lessons*. Portsmouth, NH: Heinemann.

Heffernan, N. 2003. "Helping Students Read Better: The Use of Background Knowledge." *English Teacher* 6 (1): 62–65.

History-Social Science Content Standards (Grade Four). 2006. California Department of Education. Available online at: http://www.cde.ca.gov/be/st/ss/hstgrade4.asp.

Hmong home page: http://www.hmongnet.org

Horwitz, E. 2001. "Language Anxiety and Achievement." *Annual Review of Applied Linguistics* 21: 112–26.

Johnson, D. W., and R. T. Johnson. 1995. "Why Violence Prevention Programs Don't Work—and What Does." *Educational Leadership* 52 (5): 63–68.

Keene, E. O., and S. Zimmermann. 1997. *Mosaic of Thought: Teaching Comprehension in a Reader's Workshop*. Portsmouth, NH: Heinemann.

Kohn, A. 2001. "Fighting the Tests: A Practical Guide to Rescuing Our Schools." *Phi Delta Kappan* 82 (5): 349–57.

———. 2004. *What Does It Mean To Be Well Educated? And More Essays on Standards, Grading, and Other Follies*. Boston: Beacon Press.

Krashen, S. D. 1985a. *The Input Hypothesis: Issues and Implications*. New York: Longman.

———. 1985b. *Inquiries and Insights: Second Language Teaching, Immersion and Bilingual Education, Literacy.* Hayward, CA: Alemany Press.

———. 1996. *Under Attack: The Case Against Bilingual Education.* Culver City, CA: Language Education Associates.

———. 2003. *Explorations in Language Acquisition and Use.* Portsmouth, NH: Heinemann.

———. 2004. *The Power of Reading: Insights from the Research.* 2d ed. Portsmouth, NH: Heinemann.

Krashen, S., and D. Biber. 1988. *On Course: Bilingual Education's Success in California.* Ontario, CA: California Association for Bilingual Education.

Krashen, S., and G. McField. 2005. "What Works? Reviewing the Latest Evidence on Bilingual Education." *Language Learner* 1 (2): 7–10/34.

Kroll, B. 2001. "Considerations for Teaching an ESL/EFL Writing Course." In *Teaching English as a Second Language or Foreign Language*, pp. 219–32. 3d ed. Edited by M. Celce-Murcía. Boston: Heinle & Heinle.

Nieto, S. 2004. *Affirming Diversity.* 4th ed. New York: Longman.

Odlin, T. 2003. "Cross-Linguistic Influence." In *The Handbook of Second Language Acquisition*, pp. 436–86. Edited by C. Doughty and M. Long. Malden, MA: Blackwell Publishing.

Ohio Literacy Resource Center. 2001. Available online at: http://literacy. kent.edu/NEABLE/SpeakingTerms/html/linguistics.html.

O'Malley, J. M., and L. V. Pierce. 1996. *Authentic Assessment for English Language Learners: Practical Approaches for Teachers.* Menlo Park, CA: Addison-Wesley.

Oxford, R. 1999. "Anxiety and the Language Learner: New Insights." In *Affect in Language Learning*, pp. 58–67. Edited by J. Arnold. Cambridge: Cambridge University Press.

Peterson, P. W. 2001. "Skills and Strategies for Proficient Listening." In *Teaching English as a Second Language or Foreign Language*, pp. 87–100. 3d ed. Edited by M. Celce-Murcía. Boston: Heinle & Heinle.

Ramirez, J. D. 1991. "Executive Summary of the Final Report: Longitudinal Study of Structured English Immersion Strategy, Early-exit and Late-exit Transitional Bilingual Education Programs for Language-Minority Children." In *Compendium of Research on Bilingual Education*, 1995, pp. 195–230. Edited by G. González and L. Maez. Washington, D.C.: National Clearinghouse for Bilingual Education.

Rolstad, K., K. Mahoney, and G. Glass. 2005. "The Big Picture: A Meta-Analysis of Program Effectiveness Research on English Language Learners." *Educational Policy* 19 (4): 572–94.

Rosen, N. G., and L. Sasser. 1997. "Sheltered English: Modifying Content Delivery for Second Language Learners." In *The Content-Based Classroom: Perspectives on Integrating Language and Content*, pp. 35–68. Edited by M. A. Snow and D. M. Brinton. New York: Longman.

Rubin, J., and I. Thompson. 1994. *How to be a More Successful Language Learner*. 2d ed. Boston: Heinle & Heinle.

Rumelhart, D. 1980. "Schemata: The Building Blocks of Cognition." In *Theoretical Issues in Reading Comprehension*, pp. 38–58. Edited by R. J. Spiro, B. C. Bruce, and W. F. Brewer. Hillsdale, NJ: Lawrence Erlbaum.

Schmitz, J. R. 2002. "Humor as a Pedagogical Tool in Foreign Language and Translation Courses." *Humor: International Journal of Humor Research* 15 (1): 89–113.

Seely, C., and E. Romijn. 1995. *TPR Is More Than Commands: At All Levels*. Berkeley, CA: Command Performance Language Institute.

Senechal, M., J. LeFebre, E. Hudson, and E. Lawson. 1996. "Knowledge of Storybooks as a Predictor of Young Children's Vocabulary." *Journal of Educational Psychology* 88 (1): 520–36.

Slavin, R. E. 2001. "Cooperative Learning and Intergroup Relations." In *Handbook of Research on Multicultural Education*, pp. 628–34. Edited by J. A. Banks and C. A. Banks. San Francisco: Jossey-Bass.

Slavin, R., and A. Cheung. 2005. "A Synthesis of Research on Language of Reading Instruction for English Language Learners." *Review of Educational Research* 75 (2): 247–84.

Sylwester, R. 1995. *A Celebration of Neurons: An Educator's Guide to the Human Brain*. Alexandria, VA: Association for Supervision and Curriculum Development.

Thomas, W. P., and V. P. Collier. 2002. A National Study of School Effectiveness for Language Minority Students' Long-Term Academic Achievement. CREDE (Center for Research on Education, Diversity, and Excellence). Available online at: http://crede.berkeley.edu/research/llaa/1.1_final.html.

U.S. Department of Education, Office of English Language Acquisition, Language Enhancement and Academic Achievement for Limited English Proficient Students (OELA), National Clearinghouse for

English Language Acquisition and Language Instruction Educational Programs. 2005. Available online at: www.ncela.gwu.edu/stats/2_nation.htm.

Wells, G. 1985. *Language Development in the Pre-School Years.* Cambridge: Cambridge University Press.

Western Michigan University: http//www.wmich.edu/library/access/copyright.

Williams, J. 2005. "Form-Focused Instruction." In *Handbook of Research in Second Language Teaching and Learning,* pp. 671–91. Edited by E. Hinkel. Mahwah, NJ: Lawrence Erlbaum Associates.

Wink, J. 2000. *Critical Pedagogy: Notes from the Real World.* 2d ed. New York: Allyn & Bacon.

Wolfe, P. 2001. *Brain Matters: Translating Research into Classroom Practice.* Alexandria, VA: Association for Supervision and Curriculum Development.

Wood, D. 2002. "Formulaic Language in Acquisition and Production: Implications for Teaching." *TESL Canada Journal* 20 (1): 1–15.

Trade Books Mentioned in Text

Ada, A. F. 1993. *My Name Is María Isabel*. New York: Aladdin.

Blackburn, K., and J. Lammers. 1994. *The World Record Paper Airplane Book*. New York: Workman Publishing.

Carle, E. 1996. *The Grouchy Ladybug*. New York: HarperCollins.

Cha, D. 1996. *Dia's Story Cloth: The Hmong People's Journey of Freedom*. New York: Lee & Low Books.

Collier, J. L., and C. Collier. 2005. *My Brother Sam Is Dead*. New York: Scholastic.

Gardiner, J. R. 1980. *Stone Fox*. New York: Harper & Row.

Gardiner, J. R., and A. C. W. Millet. 1996. *Stone Fox y La Carrera de Trineos*. New York: Lectorum.

Hamilton, V. 1985. *The People Could Fly: American Black Folktales*. New York: Knopf.

Mowat, F. 2001/1963. *Never Cry Wolf*. New York: Little, Brown and Company.

O'Dell, S. 1997. *Sing Down the Moon*. New York: Laurel-Leaf.

Scieszka, J., and L. Smith. 1989. *The True Story of the 3 Little Pigs!* New York: Viking.

Takahashi, R. 1998. *Inu-Yasha: A Feudal Fairy Tale* (vol. 1). San Francisco, CA: Viz Communications, Inc.

Young, E. 1989. *Lon Po Po: A Red-Riding Hood Story from China*. New York: Scholastic.

Web Resources

The Web often leaves us data rich and information poor. I recently watched a third grader interested in the history of miniature horses do a Google search on the topic. "Miniature horses" in quotes yielded 345,000 hits. Adding "history" to the search box dropped the number to 84,500. Finally, including "United States" left her with 28,500. Lots of data, but still no useable information. Teachers searching for resources for their English language learners experience the same data overload. At Google, "English language learners" produces about 1,100,000 hits. Even a highly narrowed search with the added terms "third grade," "reading compre-hension," "literature," and "assessment," means having to sift through 25,200 results. Frustrating searches like these beg the question: Now what?! One answer is to turn to annotated, topic-specific resource lists. The list below features a variety of ELL resources with an emphasis on nonprofit sites.

Directories

Directories, also known as *link banks*, do the website hunting and catego-rizing for us—a major time saver for busy teachers.

Dave's ESL Cafe Web Guide
www.eslcafe.com/search
Over 3,000 carefully categorized links, from business English, drama, and literacy, to music, pronunciation, slang, and zoos.

ESL/EFL World Directory
www.esl-eflworld.com
Nearly 700 links in forty-five categories, including three I frequently mine for authentic material for students: news online, radio online, and museums.

I Love Languages

www.ilovelanguages.com

Formerly called the Human-Languages Page. Over 2,400 links to language learning resources. Interested in learning a little—or a lot!—of your students' first languages? This is a great place to start the bilingual or multilingual journey. Over 200 language categories, including Arabic, Armenian, Hmong, Japanese, Kurdish, Somali, Spanish, Tagalog, and Yup'ik.

Isabel's ESL Site

www.isabelperez.com/tesllinks.htm

Gathered and organized by teacher Isabel Pérez Torres. Categories include grammar and writing help, pronunciation practice, testing, games, songs, webquests, and projects.

Karin's ESL Partyland Links

www.eslpartyland.com/linkspages/links.htm

Easy-to-use bank with short, helpful content descriptions for each link. Categories include interactive listening, reading on the Web, and movies and video.

Student Projects/Writing Links

http://iteslj.org/links/ESL/Student_Projects/

A mini-bank within the larger iteslj.org bank. Links to sites around the world where ESL/EFL students can exchange opinions and read and listen to work created by peers.

TESL/TEFL/TESOL/ESL/EFL/ESOL Links

http://iteslj.org/links/

Thanks to the staff at *The Internet TESL Journal* for creating and maintaining this vital, always helpful site. At last count, the master list had 13,074 links, with new sites added weekly. Welcome to Link Heaven!

TESOL/ESL/TESL Resources

www.uni.edu/becker/

Click on "TESOL/ESL" near the top of the page. Great collection of links gathered by Jim Becker, professor emeritus at the University of Northern Iowa. Sections include games and handouts, testing English skills, and help with writing.

Research and Information Centers

Center for Applied Linguistics (CAL)

www.cal.org

Based in Washington, D.C., this private, nonprofit center conducts research, develops teaching materials, and provides technical assistance and staff development in a number of areas, including ESL and bilingual education.

Center for Multilingual Multicultural Research (CMMR)

www-bcf.usc.edu/~cmmr

Research center at the University of Southern California, Rossier School of Education. Site features information on a number of important professional programs, including the USC Latino and Language Minority Teacher Projects and the Beginning Support and Assessment Induction Program for K–3 Teachers of Language Minority Students.

Center for Research on Education, Diversity, and Excellence (CREDE)

http://crede.berkeley.edu

CREDE, located at the UC Berkeley Graduate School of Education, conducts research in a number of areas, including newcomer centers, dual immersion programs, sheltered instruction, and school/community-based partnerships. Focus is on identifying and developing effective instructional approaches and strategies for linguistically and culturally diverse students.

Educational Testing Service (ETS)

www.ets.org

For information on the Test of English as a Foreign Language (TOEFL) and Test of English for International Communication (TOEIC).

Education Resources Information Center (ERIC)

www.eric.ed.gov

Sponsored by the Institute of Education Sciences (IES), U.S. Department of Education, ERIC is the mother lode for education information. The massive database contains over 1.2 million bibliographic items, from 1966 to the present, and includes journal articles, conference papers, books, policy papers, and literature reviews. ERIC regularly indexes over 600 journals. More than 100,000 full-text materials are currently available.

ESL Standards for Pre-K–12 Students (from TESOL)

www.tesol.org

Click on "Standards" under "Issues." TESOL's standards were developed collaboratively by hundreds of ESL professionals—teachers, researchers, and administrators—and designed to complement existing subject matter standards produced by other associations around the country.

Language Policy Website (James Crawford)

http://ourworld.compuserve.com/homepages/JWCrawford/

Not sure what the English Only versus English Plus debate is all about? Wondering what effects pending language legislation may have on your school or community? Looking for the latest research findings on dual immersion programs? Try James Crawford's resource rich and easy-to-navigate site. Crawford is the former Washington editor of *Education Week,* and the author of *Educating English Learners: Language Diversity in the Classroom* (2004).

National Clearinghouse for English Language Acquisition (and Language Instruction Educational Programs) (NCELA)

www.ncela.gwu.edu

Funded by the Office of English Language Acquisition, Language Enhancement and Academic Achievement for Limited English Proficient Students (OELA), U.S. Department of Education. Formerly known as the National Clearinghouse for Bilingual Education (NCBE). NCELA's easy-to-search database contains thousands of resources on program research, accountability systems, proficiency assessment, and public policy initiatives regarding the education of ELL students.

National MultiCultural Institute (NMCI)

www.nmci.org

NMCI offers conferences, workshops, and publications on workplace diversity, multicultural education, and cross-cultural conflict resolution.

Office of English Language Acquisition, Language Enhancement, and Academic Achievement for Limited English Proficient Students (OELA)

www.ed.gov/about/offices/list/oela

Previously known as the Office of Bilingual Education and Minority Languages Affairs (OBEMLA). Under the U.S. Department of Education, OELA offers program assistance and develops and disseminates national policies regarding the education of ELL students. Distributes and manages millions of dollars in Title III (formerly Title VII) grants to universities, state education agencies, districts, and schools.

Southwest Center for Education Equity and Language Diversity (SCEED)
http://sceed.asu.edu/blog

Formerly the Center for Bilingual Education Research (CBER). Housed at Arizona State University, SCEED does policy analysis and research on bilingual/dual language education.

Professional Organizations

American Association for Applied Linguistics (AAAL)
www.aaal.org

AAAL focuses on applied research in a variety of areas, including second and foreign language teaching, literacy, language assessment, and language policy.

American Council on the Teaching of Foreign Languages (ACTFL)
www.actfl.org

Top national organization for foreign language teachers. More than 9,000 members representing all grades and languages.

International Association of Teachers of English as a Foreign Language (IATEFL)
www.iatefl.org

Global community of EFL professionals. Supports and links more than 3,500 members in 100 countries through publications, conferences, and special interest groups.

International Reading Association (IRA)
www.reading.org/

One of the top literacy advocacy groups, dedicated to quality reading instruction and developing a lifelong love of reading in all students. A recent search at the site for "English Language Learners" pulled up over 200 documents.

National Association for Bilingual Education (NABE)

www.nabe.org

The premier, national-level advocacy group for bilingual education. Over 20,000 members, including bilingual/ESL teachers, paraprofessionals, administrators, parents, researchers, and public policy makers. NABE has affiliate organizations in twenty-three states. A representative sample follows. To find other state associations, go to www.nabe.org and click "About NABE," then "affiliates."

Arizona Association for Bilingual Education (AABE)
www.azbilingualed.org

California Association for Bilingual Education (CABE)
www.bilingualeducation.org

Colorado Association for Bilingual Education (CABE)
www.cobilingual.org

Illinois Association for Multicultural Multilingual Education (IAMME)
www.iamme.org

Michigan Association for Bilingual Education (MABE)
www.mabemi.org

New Mexico Association for Bilingual Education (NMABE)
www.nmabe.net

New York State Association for Bilingual Education (NYSABE)
www.nysabe.org

Texas Association for Bilingual Education (TABE)
www.tabe.org

National Association for Multicultural Education (NAME)

www.nameorg.org

Advocacy group for educational equity, social justice, and cultural pluralism through multicultural education.

The National Council of Teachers of English (NCTE)

www.ncte.org

Top-notch teacher group for English language arts education with more than 60,000 members throughout the U.S. and abroad. Special resource sections for elementary and secondary ELL students.

Teachers of English to Speakers of Other Languages (TESOL)
www.tesol.org

The preeminent international association for TESL/TEFL teachers with around 13,000 members in more than 120 countries. TESOL affiliates in the U.S., territories, and Canada:

Arizona (AZ-TESOL)
www.az-tesol.org

Arkansas (ARKTESOL)
http://wolves.dsc.k12.ar.us/arktesol/arktesol.htm

British Columbia (BCTEAL)
www.bcteal.org

California/Nevada (CATESOL)
www.catesol.org

Colorado (CoTESOL)
www.colorado.edu/iec/cotesol

Connecticut (ConnTESOL)
www.conntesol.net

Florida (SSTESOL)
www.sunshine-tesol.org

Georgia (GATESOL)
www.gatesol.org

Hawaii (Hawaii TESOL)
www.hawaiitesol.org

Illinois (ITBE)
www.itbe.org

Indiana (INTESOL)
www.intesol.org

Kansas (KATESOL/BE)
www.fhsu.edu/katesol

Kentucky (KYTESOL)
www.kytesol.org

Louisiana (LaTESOL)
www.latesol.org

Maryland (MDTESOL)
www.marylandtesol.org

Massachusetts (MATSOL)
www.matsol.org

Michigan (MITESOL)
www.mitesol.org

Minnesota (MinneTESOL)
   www.minnetesol.org
New Jersey (NJTESOL/NJBE)
   www.njtesol-njbe.org
New York State (NYSTESOL)
   www.nystesol.org
Ohio TESOL
   www.ohiotesol.org
Oklahoma (OKTESOL)
   www.oktesol.net
Ontario (TESL Ontario)
   www.teslontario.org
Oregon (ORTESOL)
   www.ortesol.org
Puerto Rico (PRTESOL)
   www.puertoricotesol.org
Quebec (SPEAQ)
   http://speaq.qc.ca
Tennessee (TNTESOL)
   www.tntesol.org
Texas (TexTESOL)
   www.textesol.org
Virginia (VATESOL)
   www.vatesol.org
Washington (WAESOL)
   www.wacsol.org
Washington, D.C. (WATESOL)
   www.watesol.org
West Virginia (WVTESOL)
   www.wvtesol.org
Wisconsin (WITESOL)
   www.witesol.org

Multistate TESOL Associations

Alabama-Mississippi (AMTESOL)
   www.amtesol.org
Idaho, Utah, Wyoming Intermountain TESOL (ITESOL)
   www.itesol.org

Iowa, Kansas, Missouri, Nebraska Mid-America (MIDTESOL)
www.midtesol.org/

Maine, New Hampshire, Vermont, Northern New England (NNETESOL)
www.nnetesol.org

North/South Carolina (Carolina TESOL)
www.carolinatesol.org

Pennsylvania (Eastern), New Jersey (Southern), Delaware (Penn TESOL-East)
www.penntesoleast.org

Western Pennsylvania, West Virginia (Three Rivers TESOL)
www.3rtesol.org

Journals

Here are some of the best online journals dealing with second language learning and teaching issues. Most are free or offer free access to articles from past issues. All get the thumbs-up from my MATESL students at the University of San Francisco.

Applied Linguistics

http://applij.oxfordjournals.org
Refereed research journal from Oxford University Press.

Bilingual Research Journal

http://brj.asu.edu
Joint project by the National Association for Bilingual Education (NABE) and the Southwest Center for Education Equity and Language Diversity (SCEED). Peer-reviewed articles.

ELT Journal

http://eltj.oxfordjournals.org
Quarterly, refereed journal from Oxford University Press.

ESL Magazine

www.eslmag.com
Articles, links, international conference schedule, and TESL/TEFL job ads from around the world.

Essential Teacher
   www.tesol.org (click on ET)
TESOL's magazine for ESL/EFL teachers and administrators, pre-K through adult education. Mainstream teachers working with ELL students will also find many helpful articles.

The Internet TESL Journal
   http://iteslj.org
Monthly journal with articles, lesson plans, and classroom materials.

JALT Journal (Japan Association for Language Teaching)
   www.jalt.org
Semiannual research journal covering a wide range of second language teaching topics. No need to be teaching English in Japan to find articles of interest!

Language Learning & Technology
   http://llt.msu.edu
Refereed journal for second and foreign language teachers. Essential reading if you're looking for more   and more effective—ways to use internet-based technology.

The Language Teacher (TLT)
   http://www.jalt-publications.org/
Monthly, peer-reviewed journal from Japan Association for Language Teaching (JALT).

TEFL Web Journal
   www.teflweb-j.org
Articles by teacher researchers.

TESL-EJ (Electronic Journal)
   http://tesl-ej.org
Launched into cyberspace in 1994, *TESL-EJ* is one of the oldest language journals on the Web. All refereed articles.

TESOL Quarterly
www.tesol.org (under Publications)
Peer-reviewed articles on a broad range of second language issues, including teacher training, curriculum development, instructional methodology, and testing and evaluation.

Activity and Material Sites

Here's a sampling of some of the best teacher- and student-tested sites on the Web. Teachers will find hundreds of activities, lessons, strategy tips, and ready-to-go materials across all grades and content areas. Students will find ESL games, puzzles, practice exercises, and mountains of authentic, high-interest listening and reading material. Some sites are ESL-specific. Others are built for native speakers but can be successfully used with ELL students with little to no modification.

BBC World Service
www.bbc.co.uk/worldservice/
Listen to the latest news and sports bulletins from around the world. The Learning English section includes articles with glossed text and downloadable programs with scripts.

Clip Art Collection for Foreign/Second Language Instruction
http://tell.fll.purdue.edu/JapanProj//FLClipart
Simple, printable line drawings. Categories include verbs, adjectives, time, and medical. Royalty free, guilt free.

Comics
GoComics
www.gocomics.com
Comics.com
www.comics.com
King Features
www.kingfeatures.com
Looking for engaging, literacy-building material for your ELL students? Try comics. These sites offer hundreds of strips and single-panel cartoons. You'll find comics for every grade and reading level. Highly recommended for your reluctant and struggling L2 readers.

Dave's ESL Cafe

www.eslcafe.com

Grab a virtual cappuccino and pull up a chair at one of the oldest ESL sites on the Web. Over the years, Dave Sperling's ESL Cafe has become the meeting spot of choice for thousands of ESL/EFL teachers and students around the world. Teacher forums include activities and games, assessment, elementary education, ESL management, literature, and video in the classroom. Student forums include computers, culture, film, hobbies, learning English, music, and pets.

English Baby!

www.englishbaby.com

Popular site with middle and high schoolers. Over 2,000 lessons featuring engaging content, discussion questions, vocabulary, and comprehension quizzes. Students can also chat in real time and make keypals with other English learners around the globe. Written material is glossed with instant definitions for tough vocabulary (simply drag the cursor over the word). Big plus: Read-along conversations and interviews, some with video, use real-world, hit-the-street English.

EnglishClub.com

www.englishclub.com

English with a British twist. Lessons on grammar, pronunciation, vocabulary. Also games, jokes, quizzes, and plenty of forums for student-to-student chat.

everythingESL.net

www.everythingesl.net

Created by ESL teacher Judie Haynes. Activity ideas, lesson plans, and Web resource suggestions.

Interesting Things for ESL Students

www.manythings.org/

A large collection of games, puzzles, and exercises for independent work, with a special section for English beginners. Material includes vocabulary games with pictures, read-and-hear jokes, and lots of quizzes on common American slang, idioms, and proverbs.

KidPub
www.kidpub.com
Online since 1995, KidPub now holds over 46,000 student-written stories. Students can read a story, add a story—or both!

Movie Trailers and Clips
ComingSoon.net
www.comingsoon.net/trailers
Apple Movie Trailers
www.apple.com/trailers
Internet Movie Database (IMDb)
www.imdb.com
English Trailers
www.english-trailers.com

Hundreds of trailers and clips to spur L2 conversation. How could a student *not* talk after watching the "Biting the Captain" clip from *Snakes on a
Plane*?! The English Trailers site is specifically designed for English language development. Each trailer is graded on comprehension level (easy,
medium, hard) and comes with warm-up questions, a short plot summary
of the movie, cloze exercise, quiz, and best of all—the full trailer script.
Developed and maintained by teacher Andrew Johnson. Thanks, Andrew!

National Public Radio (NPR)
www.npr.org
Noncommercial news, interviews, and entertainment shows. Written
transcripts available for many stories.

Voice of America
www.voanews.com/english
News and features on health, science, and American popular culture. Pod-
and webcasts in standard (authentic) English or VOA's Special English.
Special English uses short, simple sentences in active voice, free of idioms.
Announcers read Special English stories at a slightly slower pace than
standard English.

YouTube (YT)
www.youtube.com
Video clips for all grades, on every conceivable topic, with quality ranging
from the wretched to the wonderful, the tasteless to the sublime. Given

the vast number of clips to search through and the sensitive nature of some content, many teachers prefer using YT videos that they've pre-screened and organized for students in a YT Favorites Folder. There's something of interest for every student at YT. A grade 3–5 ESL teacher I recently coached had students working with videos on juggling, guinea pig care, soccer bloopers, tarantulas, magic tricks, mummies, dog training, figure skating, and spaceships.

For Younger Students

Ask for Kids

www.askforkids.com

If you've got students crying the "too-many-hits" blues, try Ask For Kids, a great starting point for webquests. Handy reference tools include a student dictionary, almanac, and world atlas. For social studies work on current events, dig into the special section on news resources for kids.

Children's Songs (Teacher's Guide)

www.theteachersguide.com/ChildrensSongs.htm

Lyrics and sound files to dozens of traditional kiddie favorites. Can't quite remember all the words to "Be Kind to Your Web-Footed Friends"? This is the place to go.

National Geographic Kids and National Geographic Little Kids

http://kids.nationalgeographic.com

http://littlekids.nationalgeographic.com

Videos, activities, stories, games, crafts, and science experiments. Kids can watch pink river dolphins, build a kaleidoscope, make a pumpkin ice cream pie, and try their hand at virtual nano surgery.

PBS Kids (Public Broadcasting Service)

http://pbskids.org

Music (with read-along lyrics), games, activities, and video clips tied to top-notch children's programs, including *Arthur, Clifford the Big Red Dog, Franny's Feet, Post Cards from Buster, Curious George, Sagwa The Chinese Siamese Cat,* and *Sesame Street.* Looking for science activities that are guaranteed language generators? Try "Build a Cantilever" or "A Boat that Floats" in the Curious George area. Some material in both English and Spanish.

List of Acronyms

It's easy to lose your footing as you wade into the literature on second language acquisition and teaching for the first time—or even the twenty-first. Suddenly, you're swimming in a churning sea of acronyms, barely able to keep your head above water.

In the book, I've kept acronyms to a bare minimum and have spelled out each one when first used. But readers swimming in other waters—other books, journals, websites, material guides, workshops, and education conferences—may find the following list helpful.

Acronyms roll in and out with the educational tide. Mercifully, a few, like PEP (Potentially English Proficient) drift out to sea and are never heard from again. The list contains mostly current terms, but also includes a few antique acronyms for readers plunging into older literature.

Safe swimming to all.

AAAL	American Association for Applied Linguistics
AAVE	African American Vernacular English
ACTFL	American Council on the Teaching of Foreign Languages
ALL	Additive Language Learning
ALM	Audiolingual Method
BAC	Bilingual Advisory Committee
BCC	Bilingual Certificate of Competence
BCLAD	Bilingual Cross-Cultural Language and Academic Development
BE	Bilingual Education
BEV	Black English Vernacular
BIA	Bilingual Instructional Assistant (Aide)
BICS	Basic Interpersonal Communicative Skills
BINL	Basic Inventory of Natural Language
BNC	Bilingual Newcomer Center
BSM	Bilingual Syntax Measures
BTTP	Bilingual Teacher Training Program
CABE	California Association for Bilingual Education

CAELA	Center for Adult English Language Acquisition
CAELD	California Assessment of English Language Development
CAH	Contrastive Analysis Hypothesis
CAI	Computer-Assisted Instruction
CAL	Center for Applied Linguistics
CALL	Computer Assisted Language Learning
CALLA	Cognitive Academic Language Learning Approach
CALP	Cognitive Academic Language Proficiency
CAT	Computer Adaptive Testing
CATESOL	California Association of Teachers of English to Speakers of Other Languages
CBER	Center for Bilingual Education and Research
CBI	Content-Based Instruction
CBLT	Competence-Based Language Teaching
CC	Communicative Competence
CELA	Center on English Learning and Achievement
CELDT	California English Language Development Test
CELTA	Certificate in English Language Teaching to Adults
CILT	Centre for Information on Language Teaching (and Research)
CLAD	Cross-Cultural Language and Academic Development
CLD	Culturally and Linguistically Diverse
CLI	Cross-Linguistic Influence
CLL	Community Language Learning
CLT	Communicative Language Teaching
CMC	Computer-Mediated Communication
CMMR	Center for Multilingual Multicultural Research
CPE	Cambridge Proficiency Examination
CREDE	Center for Research on Education, Diversity, and Excellence
CSA	Contextualized Storytelling Approach
CTEFLA	Certificate in the Teaching of English as a Foreign Language to Adults
CTEL	California Teacher of English Learners
CUP	Common Underlying Proficiency
DBAC	District Bilingual Advisory Committee
DBE	Developmental Bilingual Education
DELAC	District English Learner Advisory Committee
DELTA	Diploma in English Language Teaching for Adults
DI	Dual Immersion

DLE	Dual Language Education
DTEFLA	Diploma in the Teaching of English as a Foreign Language to Adults
EAC	Equity Assistance Center
EAL	English as an Additional Language
EAP	English for Academic Purposes
EBE	English for Business and Economics
EBP	English for Business Purposes
ED	English Dominant
EFL	English as a Foreign Language
EGI	Explicit Grammar Instruction
EGP	English for General Purposes
EIL	English as an International Language
EL	English Learner
ELA	English Language Arts
ELAC	English Learner Advisory Committee
ELAP	English Language Acquisition Program
ELD	English Language Development
ELILP	English Language and Intensive Literacy Program
ELL	English Language Learner
ELP	English for Law Purposes
ELT	English Language Teaching
EMP	English for Medical Purposes
ENL	English as a Native Language
ENL	English as a New Language
ENNL	English as a Nonnative Language
EO	English Only
EOP	English for Occupational Purposes
ERIC	Education Resources Information Center
ESD	English as a Second Dialect
ESL	English as a Second Language
ESOL	English for Speakers of Other Languages
ESPI	ELD Standards-Based Performance Indicators
ESP	English for Specific Purposes
EST	English for Science and Technology
FEP	Fluent English Proficient
FES	Fluent English Speaking
FFI	Form Focused Instruction

FLAC	Foreign Languages Across the Curriculum
FLAP	Foreign Language Assistance Program
FLES	Foreign Language in the Elementary School
FLIP	Foreign Language Incentive Program
FVR	Free Voluntary Reading
GLAD	Guided Language Acquisition Design
GTM	Grammar Translation Method
HILT	High-Intensity Language Training
HL	Heritage Language
HLE	Heritage Language Education
HLS	Home Language Survey
HOT	Higher-Order Thinking
IAAL	International Association of Applied Linguistics
IATEFL	International Association of Teachers of English as a Foreign Language
IELTS	International English Language Testing System
IEP	Intensive English Program
IFEP	Initially Fluent English Proficient
IGT	Integrative Grammar Test
IL	Interlanguage
IPA	International Phonetic Alphabet
IPT	IDEA Proficiency Test
ISE	International Standard English
L1	First/primary language
L2	Second language
LAD	Language Acquisition Device
LAS	Language Assessment Scales
LAS-O	Language Assessment Scales—Oral
LAS-R/W	Language Assessment Scales—Reading and Writing
LCD	Linguistically and Culturally Diverse
LDS	Language Development Specialist
LEA	Language Experience Approach
LEP	Limited English Proficient
LES	Limited English Speaking
LL	Language Lab
LM	Language Minority
LMS	Language Minority Student
LOTE	Language(s) Other Than English

LSP	Language for Specific Purposes
MBE	Maintenance Bilingual Education
MEP	Migrant Education Program
META	Multicultural Education Training and Advocacy
MLA	Modern Language Association
MLAT	Modern Language Aptitude Test
MTTI	Multidistrict Trainer of Trainers Institute
NAAPAE	National Association for Asian and Pacific American Education
NABE	National Association for Bilingual Education
NAME	National Association for Multicultural Education
NCBE	National Clearinghouse for Bilingual Education
NCELA	National Clearinghouse for English Language Acquisition (and Language Instruction Educational Programs)
NCLE	National Clearinghouse for (ESL) Literacy Education
NCSALL	National Center for the Study of Adult Learning and Literacy
NCTE	National Council of Teachers of English
NEP	Non-English Proficient
NES	Non-English Speaking
NEST	Native English-Speaking Teacher
NMCI	National MultiCultural Institute
NNS	Nonnative Speaker
NS	Native Speaker
OBEMLA	Office of Bilingual Education and Minority Language Affairs
OCR	Office for Civil Rights
OELA	Office of English Language Acquisition
OPI	Oral Proficiency Interview
PEP	Potentially English Proficient
PHLOTE	Primary Home Language Other Than English
PLA	Primary Language Assistant
P-L-R	Preview-Lesson-Review
PLS	Primary Language Support
P-R	Preview-Review
REST	Reading English for Science and Technology
RFEP	Redesignated Fluent English Proficient
SABE	Spanish Assessment of Basic Education

SAE	Standard American English
SAE	Student Acquiring English
SAIP	Special Alternative Instructional Program
SBI	Strategies-Based Instruction
SCLT	Sustained Content Language Teaching
SDAIE	Specially Designed Academic Instruction in English
SEI	Structured English Immersion
SEIP	Structured English Immersion Program
SET	Sheltered English Teaching
SI	Sheltered Instruction
SILL	Strategy Inventory for Language Learning
SL	Second Language
SLA	Second Language Acquisition
SLD	Second Language Development
SLE	Student Learning English
SLL	Second Language Learner
SNS	Spanish for Native Speakers
SOLOM	Student Oral Language Observation Matrix
SOPI	Simulated Oral Proficiency Interview
SPAP*	Society for the Prevention of Acronym Proliferation
SPEAK	Speaking Proficiency English Assessment Kit
SPEDLEP	Special Education Limited English Proficient
SSL	Spanish as a Second Language
SSMI	Sheltered Subject Matter Instruction
SSR	Sustained Silent Reading
SUP	Separate Underlying Proficiency
SWL	Silent Way Learning
TBE	Transitional Bilingual Education
TEAL	Teaching English as an Additional Language
TEFL	Teaching English as a Foreign Language
TESL	Teaching English as a Second Language
TESOL	Teaching English to Speakers of Other Languages
TL	Target Language
TOEFL	Test of English as a Foreign Language
TOEIC	Test of English for International Communication
TPR	Total Physical Response
TPRS	Total Physical Response Storytelling
TSE	Test of Spoken English

* My personal favorite.

TWBE	Two-Way Bilingual Education
TWE	Test of Written English
TWI	Two-Way Immersion
UG	Universal Grammar
VESL	Vocational English as a Second Language
ZPD	Zone of Proximal Development

Index